W0007578

The Sacramentary of Sarapion of Thmuis:

A Text for Students, with Introduction, Translation, and Commentary

by R. J. S. Barrett-Lennard

Chaplain and part-time lecturer in Theology in the PCD at Murdoch University, Perth, Western Australia

THE ALCUIN CLUB and the GROUP FOR RENEWAL OF WORSHIP (GROW)

The Alcuin Club, which exists to promote the study of Christian liturgy in general and of Anglican liturgy in particular, traditionally published a single volume annually for its members. This ceased in 1986 but resumed in 1992. Similarly, GROW was responsible from 1975 to 1986 for the quarterly 'Grove Liturgical Studies'. Since the beginning of 1987 the two have sponsored a Joint Editorial Board to produce quarterly 'Joint Liturgical Studies', details of which are to be found at the end of this Study.

THE COVER PICTURE

shows the location of Thmuis

First Impression September 1993
ISSN 0951-2667
ISBN 85174 246 8

GROVE BOOKS LIMITED
Bramcote   Nottingham   NG9 3DS

CONTENTS

ABBREVIATIONS

AC   *Apostolic Constitutions*
AT   *The Apostolic Tradition*
BAGD   *A Greek-English Lexicon of the New Testament and other Early Christian
         Literature*, ed. W. Bauer, W. F. Arnt and F. W. Gingrich, (2nd edn.
         Chicago University Press, Chicago, 1979)
CH   *The Canons of Hippolytus*
CHANT R. J. S. Barrett-Lennard, *Christian Healing After the New Testament: Some
         Approaches to Illness in the Second, Third and Fourth Centuries* (forthcom-
         ing, Universities Press of America, Lanham, MD, 1994)
DECA   F. X. Funk, *Didascalia et Constitutiones Apostolorum* (Vol. II. Paderborn,
         Schoeningh, 1905), pp.158-195 (Greek text)
DLW   *Dictionary of Liturgy and Worship*
LEW   F. E. Brightman, *Liturgies Eastern and Western* (Oxford University Press,
         London, 1896, reprinted 1967)
LSM   G. J. Cuming, *The Liturgy of St. Mark*, Analecta Christiana Orientialia
         234 (Pontifical Institute for Oriental Studies, Rome, Rome, 1990)
LSJ   *A Greek-English Lexicon*, ed. H. G. Liddell, R. Scott, Revd. H. S. Jones,
         Clarendon Press, Oxford, 1940. Reprint with Supplement, ed. E. A.
         Barber, Clarendon Press, Oxford, 1968
ODCC   *Oxford Dictionary of the Christian Church*
ORAC   P. Bradshaw, *Ordination Rites of the Ancient Churches of East and West*
         · (Pueblo, New York, 1990)
PGL   G. Lampe, *A Patristic Greek Lexicon* (Oxford University Press,
         London, 1961)
PTE   R. C. D. Jasper and G. J. Cuming, *Prayers of the Eucharist: Early and
         Reformed* (Collins, London, 1975, 2nd edn. 1980).
SL   G. Dix, *The Shape of the Liturgy* (Dacre Press, London, 1945)
SS   *The Sacramentary of Serapion*
TD   *Testamentum Domini*
TSL   C. Jones, G. Wainwright, E. Yarnold and P. Bradshaw, *The Study of
         Liturgy* (SPCK, London, 2nd ed. revd., 1992)
TTL   J. Cooper and A. J. Maclean (eds.), *The Testament of the Lord* (T & T
         Clark, Edinburgh, 1902 [English Translation]).

Introduction

The Sacramentary of Sarapion is a collection of thirty prayers concerning various aspects of liturgical life. In the single extant MS (Greek) they are attributed to Sarapion, the fourth-century bishop of Thmuis (339-363) in Egypt, who was a friend and confidant of Anthony and Athanasius.

IMPORTANCE OF THE TEXT

The Sacramentary is a document of very considerable liturgical interest, particularly because it appears to provide our earliest example of the Egyptian eucharistic rite. Hans Lietzmann in his classical study, *Mass and the Lord's Supper*, argued that there were two fundamental liturgical types from which all others were derived. They were a Western type and an Egyptian type of which Hippolytus (Apostolic Tradition) was the chief representative of the former and Sarapion (Sacramentary) of the latter.[1] It is now clear that the history of liturgical development in the early period is both more complex and less uniform than it appeared to Lietzmann, and some re-evaluation has been going on as to the representative value of some of our early liturgical documents such as the Apostolic Tradition.[2] However, although this re-evaluation is likely to mean that liturgical specialists may need to be more cautious about some of the conclusions they derive from these texts, our basic primary sources, of which we have comparatively so few, will remain of crucial importance. And the Sacramentary of Sarapion is one of these.

The *document* is not so much a Church Order as a manual of prayers for use by a celebrant[3], incorporating almost nothing in the way of rubrics. It includes a full anaphora, pre- and post-anaphoral prayers, five prayers relating to baptism and three to ordination and a further three prayers concerning blessing of oils, three pre-anaphoral blessings and a burial prayer. It therefore includes prayers which cover the whole spectrum of ecclesiastical services and rites.

---

[1] H. Leitzmann, *Mass and Lord's Supper: A Study in the History of the Liturgy* translated by D. H. G. Reeve with Introduction and Further Inquiry by R. D. Richardson (E. J. Brill, Leiden, 1979). The work was originally published in 1926 with the title, *Messe und Herrenmahl—Eine Studie zur Geschichte der Liturgie* (De Gruyter, Berlin). A translation of the eucharistic prayer from the Sacramentary of Sarapion is included in the collection of texts published by R. C. D. Jasper and G. J. Cuming, *Prayers of the Eucharist: Early and Reformed* (OUP, London, 1975, revised 1980), pp.38-41.

[2] See for example P. Bradshaw, *The Search for the Origins of Christian Worship* (SPCK, London, 1992).

[3] There has been some debate in the past over the proper designation of the Sacramentary. Brightman ('The Sacramentary of Serapion' in *JTS* 1 [1899-1900] 88-113; 247-277) argued it should be called not a 'Euchologion' (Wobbermin—see note 5 on p.6 below) or 'Pontifical' (Wordsworth—see note 3 on p.6 below) but a celebrant's *libellus* or 'Sacramentary' (pp.89-90). It is this latter designation that we have adopted here as the most suitable.

There is a further reason why this document is of real interest. During the last twenty years we have seen the emergence of a new focus in historical research upon the social and sociological aspects of life in the ancient world and in early Christianity. And it appears to me that scholars working with this perspective in their studies have not yet appreciated the wealth of material of this kind to be gleaned from the early liturgical documents.[1] I believe that this may reap a rich harvest.

DISCOVERY OF THE TEXT AND EARLY ASSESSMENTS OF DATE AND AUTHORSHIP[2]

The surviving MS of the Sacramentary, which includes some other writings[3], was discovered in 1894 by A. Dimitrijewsky in the library of Laura on Mt. Athos and published by him in Kiev in that year.[4] This was followed by further editions by G. Wobbermin in 1898[5], F. E. Brightman in 1899-1900[6] and F. X. Funk in 1905.[7] All these scholars were broadly in agreement that the work was at least compiled by Sarapion, bishop of Thmuis, and therefore produced in Egypt in the mid-fourth century. This dating and provenance was seen to be confirmed by internal evidence from the document itself.[8]

In contrast to Wobbermin who had argued that the text attributed only two of the prayers to Sarapion, Brightman suggested that it actually attributed at least five of the prayers to him[9] and he took the view that there was no reason why the

[1] I have attempted something of this kind of my forthcoming study, *Christian Healing After the New Testament: Some Approaches to Illness in the Second, Third and Fourth Centuries* (University Press of America, Lanham, MD, 1994). In addition to examining this theme in papyrus letters and Patristic writers, the work also explores these ideas in the Apostolic Tradition and the Sacramentary of Sarapion.

[2] In this section I am using some material from pp.277-284 of my study, *Christian Healing After the New Testament*, referred to in note 1 above. It is used with permission of the University Press of America, Copyright, 1994.

[3] See J. Wordsworth, *Bishop Sarapion's Prayer Book: An Egyptian Sacramentary dated Probably about A.D. 350-356* (SPCK, London, 1910), pp.9-10.

[4] A. Dimitrijewsky, *Ein Euchologium aus dem 4. Jahrhundert, verfasstg von Sarapion, Bischof von Thmuis* (Kiev, 1894).

[5] G. Wobbermin, *Altchristlich liturgische Stücke aus der Kirche Aegytens nebst einem dogmatischen Brief des Bischofs Sarapion von Thmuis*, TU 18, 3b (Hinrichs, Leipzig, 1898).

[6] F. E. Brightman, 'The Sacramentary of Serapion', *op. cit.*

[7] Funk, *Didaskalia et Constitutiones Apostolorum*, Vol. II, (Schoeningh, Paderborn, 1905), pp.158-195.

[8] See Brightman, 'The Sacramentary of Serapion', pp.90-93.

[9] The difference of opinion arose from the fact that the word *proseuchē* in the title to No. 15 (the numbering system followed in this publication is that of the Brightman text not Funk) is contracted to *proseuch* (see Funk, *Didaskalia*, Vol. II, p.xli). Wobbermin assumed the contraction was of the singular, *proseuchē*, whereas Brightman ('The Sacramentary of Serapion', p.60) saw Nos. 15-18 as being a closely related unit of prayers and read the plural *proseuchai*. B. Botte in his article, 'L'Eucologe de Sérapion est-il authentique?' in *Oriens Christianus* 48 (1964) 50-56 seems to feel that the argument is evenly balanced (p.50, note 2).

collection of prayers should not 'in whole or part, be the work of Sarapion'.[1] A similar position was taken by Bishop John Wordsworth in his publication of the first English translation of the text in 1899 and in his later revision of 1910[2] which drew upon Brightman's work.

MORE RECENT WORK ON DATE AND AUTHORSHIP

Since the Second World War there have been a number of articles dealing with the questions of the date, author (and provenance) of the Sacramentary. In 1945 Dom B. Capelle published an article entitled, 'L'Anaphore de Sérapion: essai d'exégèse'.[3] He accepted that Sarapion was responsible for the collection of prayers and suggested that where he drew upon earlier materials, such as in the anaphora, he moulded them in accordance with his own presuppositions and ideas with the result that the work, as we have it, exhibits a substantial unity.[4] Capelle did not call into question the traditional mid-fourth century date for the Sacramentary but he saw Sarapion as an innovator and therefore concluded that the work was not a very reliable source for information about wider Egyptian liturgical traditions of this period.[5]

Nearly twenty years later, Dom Botte examined the work in an article entitled, 'L'Eucologe de Sérapion est-il authentique?'.[6] Botte concluded that the extant work betrayed a definite Arian tendency and represented a reworking of Sarapion's prayers by an astute Arian or person of Arian sympathies who was also a Pneumatomachian, fifty to one hundred years later than the generally accepted date of c. A.D. 350.[7] Botte sees the regular use of the phrase 'holy Spirit' in the doxologies without a definite article, the lack of reference to the Spirit in the blessing of the oil of the sick and the fact that the epiclesis in the anaphora is of the Word and not the Spirit, as evidence that the redactor betrays an unorthodox doctrine of the Spirit.[8] He also argues that the use of the term 'uncreated' (agenētos—rather than agennētos) to refer to the Father and 'only-begotten' (monogenēs) to describe the Son indicates a subordinationist tendency in his doctrine of the Son.[9]

Some of these ideas have been developed in a privately published German monograph on the Pneumatomachians by H. D. Hauschild.[10] This writer also

---

[1] Brightman, 'The Sacramentary'. p.90.
[2] Details cited in note 3 on p.6 opposite.
[3] B. Capelle, 'L'Anaphore de Sérapion: essai d'exégèse' in *Le Muséon* 59 (1946) 425-443 [reprinted in *Travaux liturgiques* 2 (1962) 344-358].
[4] *Ibid.*, p.438.
[5] *Ibid.*, pp.438-443.
[6] B. Botte, 'L'Eucologe de Sérapion est-il authentique?' in *Oriens Christianus* 48 (1964) 50-56.
[7] *Ibid.*, pp.51 and 55.
[8] *Ibid.*, pp.53-55.
[9] *Ibid.*, pp.52-53.
[10] W. D. Hauschild, *Die Pneumatomachen: Eine Untersuchung zur Dogmengesch-ichte des vierten Jahrhunderts* (Hamburg, 1967), pp.153-169. This work was a doctoral dissertation accepted by the Protestant Faculty of Theology in the University of Hamburg. I am grateful to Michael Colbacher of Heidelberg for drawing my attention to it.

argues that the document reflects both a diminution in the role of the Spirit which he calls 'binitarian monotheism' and a doctrine of the Son which locates him with writers he describes as moderate Arians such as Eusebius of Caesarea, Theodore of Heraklea and Eusebius of Emesa.[1] He develops this last point with reference to what he calls an *agennētos-monogenēs*' schema which he finds in both the *Sacramentary* and these writings of the moderate Arians.[2] Although he gives a more or less traditional dating for the Sacramentary, he takes it to be, in its current form, the work of a redactor whose theological milieu is Syrian rather than Egyptian.[3]

I do not find Hauschild's position very plausible and I have attempted to show why elsewhere.[4] And in doing so I have been influenced by an important article published in 1980 by G. J. Cuming[5] which seeks to respond to the earlier articles by Capelle and particularly Botte whose assessment of the Sacramentary had in the meantime gained some support.

Cuming's article is an attempt to rehabilitate the place of the Sacramentary as well as to propose a new understanding of the correct order of the prayers. He challenged Botte's arguments at several key points showing that the alleged Arianism of the final editor is by no means proved.[6] Cuming demonstrates that in the letters of Athanasius concerning the Holy Spirit which he wrote to Sarapion, Athanasius himself sees the Spirit and the Logos as very closely linked together.[7] He suggests therefore that Athanasius and Sarapion would see an epiclesis of the Logos as also involving the Spirit and that in this respect the doctrine of the Spirit in the prayers is orthodox by the standards of the first half of the fourth century.[8]

Cuming also examines the question of the use of the term *agenētos* in the Sacramentary and suggests that, in view of the frequent scribal confusion between this term and the term *agennētos*, a scribe many centuries later may have readily confused the two, reading *agenētos* for an original *agennētos*.[9] He notes that this

---

[1] Hauschild, *Die Pneumatomachians*, p.164.
[2] *Ibid.*, pp.163-164. He is apparently developing the argument of Botte ('L'Eucologe de Sérapion est-il authentique?', pp.51-53), although the force of Botte's argument was dependent upon what he saw as subordinationism in the Sacramentary's use of the term *agenētos*. Hauschild actually reads the term *agenētos* and does so consistently, when the Sacramentary in fact has the word *agenētos*. And though Cuming has suggested that the original may indeed have been *agennētos* (Cuming, 'Thmuis Revisited', p.574), Hauschild gives no explanation for this change. Presumably, though, Hauschild believes the original was *agennētos*.
[3] Hauschild, *Die Pneumatomachians*, pp.154-165.
[4] See Barrett-Leonard, *Christian Healing, op. cit.*, pp.271-273.
[5] G. J. Cuming, 'Thmuis Revisited: Another Look at the Prayers of Bishop Sarapion' in *TS* 41 (1980) 568-575.
[6] *Ibid.*, p.573-574.
[7] *Ibid.*, p.573.
[8] *Ibidem.*
[9] *Ibid.*, p.574. The confusion between the terms is noted by Lampe, *A Patristic Greek Lexicon* (OUP, London, 1961) under the entries for *agenētos* and *agennētos*.

gives better sense because it is the true opposite of the term *monogenēs*—'unbegotten' contrasted with 'only-begotten'—and observes that the opposite of *agenētos*, the word *genētos* 'created', is never applied to the Son. Though an argument from silence, he suggests that the possibility of this simple error having occurred seriously weakens Botte's position.[1]

Cuming brings forward some further evidence from the anaphora to suggest an earlier rather than a later date for the collection and concludes the article noting that, 'it becomes increasingly possible that the collection and editing of the prayers was the work of Sarapion, Bishop of Thmuis and friend of Athanasius.'[2] Cuming, in his *The Liturgy of St. Mark* (published posthumously in 1990)[3], has indicated that scholarly opinion has now turned back in favour of the prayers being associated with Sarapion, the friend of Athanasius, and he cites in support of this the work of Bouyer and Betz.

This is essentially also the position taken in an earlier monograph on the Sacramentary published in 1967 by P. E. Rodopoulos, a Greek Orthodox scholar.[4] Rodopoulos accepted both the mid-fourth century dating and that Bishop Sarapion was either the author or redactor of the work.[5] Rodopolous' study also includes a reproduction of the Brightman Greek text of the Sacramentary but no translation.

The view adopted here is that while there must remain a real element of uncertainty until further detailed work is done on the text, the case against associating the prayers with Sarapion, Bishop of Thmuis, has not been established. Sarapion can still be credited with at least the collection and perhaps the editing of the prayers and if so they must be dated somewhere between 339 and c.360 AD. Brightman thought them not later than 350 and if we associate Sarapion of Thmuis with the work then Brightman's careful analysis of the internal criteria, including theology, the doxologies and the ecclesiastical conditions of the time, has not been superseded.[6]

THE ORDER (AND NUMBERING) OF THE PRAYERS

The prayers of the Sacramentary are not numbered in the MS and this has led to some confusion as to their proper order, particularly because there is wide agreement that their order in the MS is most unlikely to have been the original order. It has also led to the development of two separate numbering systems. Wobbermin printed them in the order in which they occur in the MS, giving a Roman numeral to each one sequentially. Wordsworth repeated this order, giving each

---

[1] *Ibidem.*

[2] *Ibid.*, p.575.

[3] G. J. Cuming, *The Liturgy of St. Mark*, Orientalia Christiana Analecta 234 (Pontifical Institute for Oriental Studies, Rome, 1990), pp.xxxvi-xxxvii.

[4] P. E. Rodopoulos, *The Sacramentary of Serapion* (no publisher given, Thessalonika, 1967).

[5] *Ibid.*, pp.26-36. Rodopoulos is willing to countenance the idea that the work may even be earlier than mid-fourth century, see p.36.

[6] Brightman, 'The Sacramentary', pp.91-93. Cuming, *The Liturgy of St. Mark, op. cit.*, p.xxxvi, suggests a date of between '350 and 360 A.D. (note the printer's error there '250' for '350').

prayer a sequential (Arabic) number. Brightman however argued that the prayers were not in their correct order and, while he preserved the same numbering system, he re-arranged the placement of the prayers to suit what he took to be their most logical order. Brightman's order is:

The Liturgy, 19-30, 1-6
The Order of Baptism and Confirmation, 7-11, 15, 16
Ordinations, 12-14
Unction of the Sick, 17
Burial of the Dead, 18

This sounds rather like the order of services in the Anglican Book of Common Prayer! However Funk, in publishing his edition of the Greek text in 1905, retained the order that Brightman had suggested, but now renumbered all the prayers sequentially in the Brightman order. He used Greek numbering for the Greek of the prayers and a large Roman numeral for each prayer of the parallel Latin translation, next to which was placed a further smaller Roman number in brackets corresponding to the MS order of the prayers.

Both numbering systems seem to be in use, with Continental scholars tending to use Funk's system and British/American scholars tending to use the Brightman system. This matter calls for a resolution but it may have to await the much-needed fresh critical edition of the work.

In this edition I have followed the Brightman system of numbering and his order though only because it is the order of both the Brightman and Funk Greek texts. As noted below, Cuming, while using the Brightman system of numbering, has made a further suggestion as to the possible original order of the prayers and in my view it has much to commend it.

In his article to which reference has already been made, Cuming took issue with Brightman in his view that the prayers were not arranged in any logical order.[1] He put forward the ingenious suggestion that the copyist who made our extant MS in the eleventh century placed the second half of the work before the first half, an error which could well have occurred if the earlier codex was in a dilapidated state.[2] Cuming contended that a simple reversal of the two halves of the extant work results in an essentially natural and logical order of contents.[3] His corrected order is then:

Preliminary blessings of oils (15-17)
A burial prayer (18)
The Eucharist (19-30, 1-6)
Baptism (7-11)
Ordination (12-14)[4]

---

[1] Brightman, 'The Sacramentary of Serapion', p.89.
[2] Cuming, 'Thmuis Revisited', p.568-569.
[3] Ibid., p.570-571. He notes though that there are still 'a few rough places to be made plain' (p.570). The re-arrangement of the text proposed by Brightman has, more often than not, been followed in later editions, including that of Funk (although Funk establishes a new system of numbering the prayers). However, J. Wordsworth in his English translation, retained the existing order of the MS.
[4] Cuming, 'Thmuis Revisited', p.570.

Such change also means that the title which occurs between Prayers 14 and 15[1]—'Prayer(s) of Sarapion, Bishop of Thmoueis' may well be a general title for the whole collection. This is further suggested by the fact that there is a separate specific title for Prayer 15 which relates to the theme of that prayer.[2] There is a title incorporating Sarapion's name in the anaphora (Prayer 1) but it is the only title at that point and relates to the theme of the anaphora. Cuming adduces evidence from the Coptic version of the Liturgy of St Mark for the use of such a subordinate title before an anaphoral prayer.

In the view of Cuming therefore, the scribal copyist may have mistaken the title associated with the anaphora as the title of the whole work and hence placed that prayer first in the collection. This seems to be confirmed, he suggests, by an annotation on the MS after Prayer 30 where the scribe has written 'All these prayers are to be said before the anaphora.'[3]

Cuming argues that the work is in fact 'carefully and logically arranged'[4] though he does not believe that the original prayers are all from the same hand. He suggests that Capelle and other earlier students of the work had been too ready to accept its homogeneity and he argues that the collection is actually made up of several groups of prayers.[5]

THIS TRANSLATION

This translation is a fresh translation of the Greek text. Any translator must steer a course between an overly literal rendering and one which removes the reader too far from the feel of the original. I have sought to make a translation which is smooth and reads easily but which also remains reasonably close to the original. In completing the work I have compared my readings with Wordsworth's translation for whose work I have considerable admiration and at times I have been influenced by his judgment.

---

[1] The title reads, *Proseuch. sarapionos episkopou thmouseos* (I. *thmoueos*) (Brightman, 'Sacramentary', p.89 and Funk, *Didaskalia*, Vol. II, p.xli).

[2] See Cuming, 'Thmuis Revisited', pp.569-570.

[3] Brightman, 'Sacramentary', p.89 and Funk, *Didaskalia*, Vol., 2, p.166, note 1.

[4] Cuming, 'Thmuis Revisited', p.571.

[5] *Ibid.*, p.572.

Translation

We beseech you, the Father of the only-begotten, the Lord of the universe, the creator of all that has been created, the maker of hte things that have been made; we stretch out clean hands and we open up our minds to you, Lord. Have compassion, we pray, deal leniently with us, do good to us, improve us and increase in us virtue and faith and knowledge. Have regard[1] for us, Lord; we offer up to you our own weaknesses. Be gracious to us and have mercy upon us all together. Have mercy upon this people; do good to us; enable us to have gentleness and prudence and purity and send angelic powers upon us in order that this your people may be truly holy and worthy. And I beseech you, send holy Spirit into

---

[1] Gk. *episkepsai ēmas* cf. Ps. 105.4 (All references to the Psalms are to the LXX version).

---

[19] As noted in the Introduction, p.10 above, Brightman rearranged the MS order of the prayers placing this one first. In the view of Cuming ('Thmuis Revisited', pp.568-570) the MS actually began with the title 'Prayer(s) of Sarapion, Bishop of Thmoueis', followed by three preliminary blessings of oils (Ns. 15-17).

Prayers 19-30 appear to be all pre-anaphoral prayers (see Wordsworth, *BSPB*, p.80) used in the Liturgy of the Word.

This particular prayer, which would begin the eucharistic liturgy, appears to be a feature of Egyptian liturgies and somewhat similar prayers are found in the Liturgy of St. Mark (Cuming, *LSM*, pp.5-6: 88-90) and the closely related Liturgy of the Coptic Jacobites (*LEW*, p.147). Cuming in his suggested structure of the first part of the Liturgy of St. Mark places the 'First Prayer of the Morning' at the beginning of the pre-anaphoral section. The Canons of Hippolytus (ET: ed. P. Bradshaw, Grove Joint Liturgical Studies no 2, 1987), which appears to come from an area not far from Thmuis and may be of a very similar date (336-340 AD, see Bradshaw, *The Canons*, p.7 where he draws on the work of René-Georges Coquin), does not include such a prayer. However like its precursor, the Apostolic Tradition, it does not include any comprehensive eucharistic rite.

–send holy Spirit]. One of the features of these prayers is the omission of the definite article in nearly all references to the Holy Spirit (except Prayers 10, 16 and 13) which has led to debate as to whether the prayers reflect an orthodox view of the Spirit (see Introduction pp.7-8). Cuming in his article 'Thmuis Revisited' does not deal with the specific issue of the use of *agion pneuma*, but he does argue that in relation to the epiclesis of the Word (rather than Spirit), the doctrine of the Spirit is not unorthodox. This use may merely reflect an undeveloped doctrine of the Spirit in a period prior to the Pneumatomachian or Macedonian controversy. This would in fact be consistent, if Sarapion was responsible for the final form of the prayers, with Athanasius writing his letters to Sarapion concerning the Holy Spirit. And in *Epist. ad Serap.*, 1, 4, Athanasius himself does not insist on the use of the definite article where an attribute of the Holy Spirit is used (such as holy) but he does otherwise. Wordsworth (*BSPB*, p.19) suggests that the omission of the article, at least in the doxologies, would not have been unacceptable to Athanasius. And in the doxology at the conclusion of his *de incarn.*, 57 Athanasius uses the phrase 'in holy Spirit'.

our minds and grant us to learn the divine scriptures from holy Spirit and inter-
pret them correctly and worthily, that all the people present may benefit,
through your only-begotten Jesus Christ in holy Spirit, through whom to you be
the glory and the power both now and to all the ages of ages. Amen.

[20] PRAYER AFTER STANDING UP AFTER THE SERMON
God the Saviour, God of the universe, the Lord and creator of the whole world,
the begetter of the only-begotten who has begotten the true[1] and living image,

---

[1] Gk. *chàractēra*, cf. Heb. 1.3.

–learn the divine scriptures]. This prayer led into the Scripture readings which were
   an element of the pre-eucharistic services at least as early as Justin (1 *Apol.*, 67)
   and almost certainly earlier. In the Liturgy of St. Mark there are several further
   prayers before the readings (*LSM*, pp.vii, 12-13, 97-98). See further P. Cobb, *TSL*,
   pp.225-227.
–through your only-begotten]. This doxology is used at the end of every prayer except
   the anaphora (N.1) where it is significantly altered. There are small differences in
   Ns. 3, 6, 18 and 25. The doxologies consistently use the pattern 'to the Father,
   through the Son, in holy Spirit' rather than the coordinate for 'to . . . to . . . to'.
   The use here appears to be a primitive form which appears in some other texts
   including the liturgy of *AC*, 7.45, 48; 8.5; 6; 8; 9; 11 but quickly dropped out of
   use when the Arians began to argue that it indicated the inferiority of the Son
   and Spirit. Brightman ('Sacramentary', pp.92 and 108) notes that it occurs
   occasionally in Athanasius (see e.g. *de incarn.*, 57; *ad. episc., Egypt et Lib.*, 23; *de
   fuga*, 27 and *hist. Arian.*, 80). *AT* consistently has 'with the Holy Spirit' in its
   doxologies as do some of the later prayers in the liturgy of *AC. CH* uses a number
   of variations but twice the form 'through our Lord Jesus Christ, through whom
   be glory to you, with him and the Holy Spirit, to the ages of ages' (Canons 5, 19).
   The whole question of the use of the prepositions in reference to the Trinity was
   taken up by St. Basil in *de Spiritu sancto* where he sought to respond to the
   Pneumatomachian understanding of the doxologies and of the Holy Spirit. See
   further Wordsworth, *BSBP*, pp.17-19.
–only-begotten]. Gk *monogenēs*. This term occurs in every prayer and sometimes
   more than once (50 times in all).

[20] Title: The SS has almost nothing in the way of specific rubrics. However the titles
of the prayers are sometimes specific titles and sometimes titles with additional
information of the kind associated with rubrics, such as we have here (cf. Ns. 2-4, 11,
16, 18). Brightman ('Sacramentary', p.94) notes that this prayer seems to have been
dropped in the Greek Liturgy of St. Mark but has some parallel in the Coptic and
Abyssian rites (*LEW*, pp.157, 220) and the Greek St. James (*LEW*, p.38). It is also
illustrated by the words 'let us arise and pray' in some of Origen's sermons (*in Numb.*
20.5; *in Esai* 3.3; *in Luc.* 36, 39; see further see Brightman, 'Sacramentary', p.109).
   The sermon generally came after the Gospel reading and by the fourth century in
the East there was often more than one sermon as the bishop may invite all the presbyters who wished to preach to do so and then he himself would preach. (*AC*, 2.57.9;
Egeria, 25.1). See further *TSL*, p.187 and *LEW*, p.588.

who sent him for the benefit of the human race[1] and who, through him, called and won over humanity, we pray to you on behalf of this people. Send holy Spirit and let the Lord Jesus visit them; let him speak to the minds of everyone and let him prepare in advance their hearts for faith. God of mercies may he himself draw their souls to you in order to acquire[2] a people even in this city; to acquire[3] a genuine flock, through your only-begotten Jesus Christ in holy Spirit, through whom to you be the glory and the power both now and to all the ages of ages. Amen.

[21] PRAYER FOR THE CATECHUMENS

Helper and Lord of all, deliverer of those who have been delivered, protector of those who have been rescued, the hope of those who have come under your powerful hand. You are the one who has destroyed lawlessness, who through the only-begotten has rendered Satan impotent and destroyed his handiwork and released those who had been bound by him. We give you thanks for the catechumens, because you have called them through the only-begotten and you freely gave to them your knowledge.[4]

And therefore we pray, let them be firmly established in this knowledge[4] in order that they may know you the only true God and him whom you sent, Jesus Christ.

May they be protected in the things they have learnt and in pure wisdom and may they prosper to become worthy of the washing of regeneration and of the holy mysteries[5], through the only begotten Jesus Christ in holy Spirit, through whom to you be the glory and the power both now and to all the ages of ages. Amen.

---

[1] The Gk. *anthrōpos* has been consistently translated inclusively.
[2] MS here *ktēsai* not *ktisai*. [4] Gk. *gnōsis.*
[3] MS has *ktisa* but Brightman reads *ktēsai.* [5] Gk. *hagia mystēria.*

–to acquire a people . . . to acquire a genuine flock]. Brightman's reading (also Funk, *DECA*, Vol II, p.160) *ktēsai* is paralleled in the Liturgy of St. Mark (Cuming, *LSM*, p.23; *LEW*, p.126) and may derive from Is. 26.13.

[21]: This prayer and N.28 concern catechumens. At least since the time of Justin (1 *Apol.*, 65) those who were not baptized (and penitents also) had to leave the Christian gathering before the Prayers and the Kiss of Peace (see Cobb, *TSL*, p.288). By the time of *AT*, the catechumens first pray by themselves after the sermon, then 'the teacher' lays his hands on them, prays and dismisses them (*AT*, 18, 19). In *CH*, 18, 30 the regulations relating to the catechumens are somewhat misplaced but the procedure seems to be very similar to that of *AT* and we know that in the East a similar pattern was being followed by the fourth century (cf. *AC*, 8.6 and Chrysostom, in *2. Cor. hom.*, 2.5). Further information is given in Canon 19 of the Canons of Laodicea which may date from c.365 AD (cited by Wordsworth, *BSPB*, p.34).

–under your powerful hand]. 1 Pet. 5.6. The expression occurs also in N.16 and cf. 3, 10, 26, 29, 30.
–released those . . . bound]. Lk. 13.16.
–that they may know you . . . Jesus Christ]. Jn. 17.3.
–washing of regeneration]. Tit. 3.5. This phrase is also used in N.16.
–in pure wisdom]. Gk *katharai phronēsei*. The term *karathos* is a very frequent one in the prayers. It has generally been rendered here as 'pure' rather than 'clean' as Wordsworth had done.

We stretch out our hand, Master, and we pray that your divine and living hand may be stretched out in blessing on this people. For they bow their heads to you, uncreated Father, through the only-begotten. Bless this people with a blessing of knowledge and godliness and with a blessing of your mysteries, through your only-begotten Jesus Christ, through whom to you be the glory and the power in holy Spirit both now and to all the ages of ages. Amen.

---

[28]: This prayer represents a special blessing for the catechumens before their departure from the assembly (see Cobb, *TSL*, p.228). Canon 19 of the Canons of Laodicea specifically refers to penitents coming forward for laying on of hands by the bishop before their departure. Wordsworth (*BSPB*, pp.52-53) suggests that originally an actual laying on of hands would have been involved in all the prayers of blessing but that increasing numbers eventually led to the substitution of merely an outstretched hand. By the time of Augustine, he can write 'what is the laying on of hands except prayer over a man' (*de bapt. contra Don.*, 3.16). See further *CHANT*, pp.308-309.

Within the liturgy this prayer would represent the completion of the Liturgy of the Word with the dismissal of the catechumens following (cf. *AT*, 19 and *CH*, 18). Such a dismissal is still found in the Byzantine rite (*TSL*, p.229).

In Cuming's rearrangement this prayer actually comes later in the MS order after the pre-anaphoral prayers. In his view it is placed there to group it with two other prayers of blessing, Ns. 29, 30 ('Thmuis Revisited', pp.568-570).

-Title—Laying on of Hands]. Gk. *cheirothesia*. This term is used in Ns. 3, 6, 28, 29, 30 and it is difficult to know whether it is best rendered 'blessing' as Cuming has done in his titles in the article 'Thmuis Revisited' (pp.568-5690 or more literally, as here. I have adopted the latter rendering to bring out the hisotrical emphasis within the phrase and to avoid any danger of a simplistic association of the term 'blessing' in these contexts with the 'blessing' in contemporary liturgies of today. See further C.II. Turner, '*Cheirotonia, cheirothesia, epithesis cheirōn*' in *JTS* 24 (1922-23) 496-504 and discussion in *CHANT*, pp.307-309 and Lampe, *PGL*, s.v. *cheirothesia*.

-living hand]. The term 'living' (Gk. participle, *zōn*) is a frequent one in the prayers, along with 'life' (*zōē*). The use of 'hand' in reference to God is also common (Ns. 3, 10, 16, 29, 30).

-uncreated Father]. Gk. *agenētos* (possibly originally *agennētos*—see Introduction pp.8-9). This is another very characteristic term in the prayers (Ns. 1, 3, 5, 7, 13, 26, 27).

[27] PRAYER FOR THE PEOPLE

We make confession to you, humanity-loving God, and we hand over our weaknesses and we pray that strength may be added to us. Pardon our earlier sins and forgive all the past faults and make us new people. Cause us also to be genuine and pure servants. We dedicate ourselves to you; receive us, O God of truth, receive this people. Grant this whole people to be genuine; grant this whole people to conduct themselves blamelessly and with purity. Let them be numbered with the heavenly ones, let them be counted with the angels, and let them become fully elect and holy.

We beseech you on behalf of those who have believed and have come fully to know the Lord Jesus Christ; let them be firmly established in the faith and in the knowledge and the teaching.

We pray for this people; be reconciled to all; make yourself known; reveal your radiance. Let them all know you, the uncreated Father, and your only-begotten Son Jesus Christ.

We pray for all rulers; let them have a peaceful life, for the sake of the tranquillity of the catholic Church.

We pray, God of mercies, for those who are free and for slaves, for men and women; for the old men and children, for the poor and the rich. Show kindness to all your own family and stretch out your hands to all your own people in benevolence. Have compassion on all and grant to all conversion to you.

---

[27]: Justin (*1 Apol.*, 65) makes it clear that after baptism the first act of the former catechumens was to participate in the prayers of the faithful. And this is paralleled in *AT*, 21 (Cuming, p.21), [*TSL*, p.229].

In the outline of the liturgy of *SS* by Wordsworth (*BSPB*, pp.36-39), he envisages this prayer, N.27, being preceded by N.29 (Laying on of Hands of the People), N.22 (Prayer for those who are Sick), N.30 (Laying on of hands of the Sick), N.23 (Prayer for Harvest), N.24 (Prayer for the Church), N.25 (Prayer for the Bishop of the Church) and N.26 (Prayer of Bending the Knee). This is very similar to Cuming's order ('Thmuis Revisited', pp.568-570) except that it appears that he would have envisaged N.29 (Laying on of Hands of the People) coming straight after N.27 (just as N.28 would come after N.21) as, in fact, Brightman did, and hence N.29 follows this prayer in the current order.

-new people]. Ephes. 4.24.
-O God of truth]. Ps. 30.6.
-firmly established in the faith]. Col. 2.7.
-make yourself known]. Jn. 17.3.
-all rulers]. Wordsworth (*BSPB*, pp.12-13) suggests the very short and reserved prayer for 'rulers' indicates the reign of Constantius and accordingly he dates the whole work 350-356 AD.
-for the . . . tranquillity . . .]. In contrast to Wordsworth, it is better not to take this as a separate petition (see Brightman, 'Sacramentary', p.109).

We beseech you on behalf of those travelling; grant to them a peaceful angel to be a companion on the way, that they suffer no harm by anyone, that they may finish the voyage and their travels in great contentment.

We beseech you on behalf those who are afflicted and in prison and in poverty; relieve each of them, deliver them from their bonds, bring them out of poverty, comfort all—you who are the comforter and consoler.

We pray for those who are sick; grant them health and raise them up from their sickness and enable them to have perfect health of body and soul.

For you are the Saviour and benefactor; you are the Lord and King of all. We have called upon you on behalf of all, through your only-begotten Jesus Christ, through whom to you be the glory and the power in holy Spirit both now and to all the ages of ages. Amen.

[29] LAYING ON OF HANDS OF THE LAITY

Let the living and pure hand, the hand of the only-begotten, the one that has torn apart all evil things and firmly established and safeguarded all holy things[1], be

---

[1] Gk. *ta hagia.*

–peaceful angel]. Brightman 'Sacramentary', p.110), draws attention to parallels to this phrase in Chrysostom and elsewhere.

–for those who are sick]. Concern for the sick and prayer for healing is a marked feature of a number of the prayers of *SS* (Ns. 5, 15, 17, 22; see *CHANT*, pp.227-323) and is reflected in several Canons of *CH* (Ns. 3, 5, 8, 21, 24, 25, 30; I examined this theme in *CH* in an as yet unpublished paper presented to the International *SBL* Conference in Melbourne (Aust.) in 1992.) This concern is reflected in many ancient liturgies but may be particularly prominent in Egyptian liturgies, cf. the Liturgy of St. Mark (Cuming, *LSM*, pp.23-24; *ET*, p.71; *LEW*, pp.119, 126 and the Liturgy of the Coptic Jacobites (*LEW*, p.166).

–Lord and King]. Brightman ('Sacramentary', p.110) suggests this may be a distinctive Egyptian expression.

[29]: This prayer, along with Ns. 28 and 30, form a group of prayers for laying on of hands/blessings. Whereas in N.28 the catechumens are prayed for that they might receive a blessing of 'knowledge, godliness and your mysteries', here the request is for laity to receive the blessing of 'the Spirit, heaven and that of the prophets and apostles' in addition to the requests for the catechumens. The emphasis on blessing is very marked. There is also a strong emphasis in this prayer on moral purity.

Brightman notes ('Sacramentary', p.110) that this prayer is not found in other Egyptian liturgies but has some parallel in Syrian rites (*LEW*, pp.12, 30, 44, 84).

–torn apart . . . evil things]. Presumably a reference to the cross/resurrection and its effect.

–holy things]. The reference is unclear but it may be simply a general affirmation.

stretched out over the heads of this people. May this people be blessed with the blessing of the[1] Spirit, with the blessing of heaven, and with the blessing of the prophets and apostles. May the bodies of the people be blessed for self-control and purity. May their souls be blessed for learning and knowledge and the mysteries.[2] May they all be blessed in common, through your only-begotten Jesus Christ, through whom to you be the glory and the power in holy Spirit both now and to all the ages of ages. Amen.

[22] PRAYER FOR THE SICK

We beseech you, the overseer and Lord and modeller of the body and maker of the soul, the one who constructed humanity, the governor[3] and guide[4] and saviour of every race of humanity, the one who is reconciled[5] and appeased[6] because of your own benevolence. Be gracious, Master; help and heal all who are sick. Rebuke the sicknesses; raise up those who are bed-ridden; give glory to your holy name, through your only-begotten Jesus Christ, through whom to you be the glory and the power in holy Spirit both now and to all the ages of ages. Amen.

---

[1] 'the' supplied.
[2] Gk. *ta mystēria*.
[3] Gk. *oikonomos*.
[4] Gk. *kybernētē*.
[5] Gk. *katallosoomenos*.
[6] Gk. *praynomenos*.

–the bodies . . . be blessed . . . souls be blessed]. The use of both these terms seems to be evidence of an emphasis in *SS* upon the effect of the divine working upon the whole person, cf. N.15 'soul, body and spirit' and the end of the anaphora N.1, and Ns. 2, 6, 22.

–the mysteries]. The term probably has the Eucharist and other rites in mind, cf. Ns. 3, 6, 8.

[22]: As noted above (N.27), there is a marked emphasis upon ministry to the sick in *SS*. Coupled with the interest in the theme in *CH* as well it suggests that a concern about illness and healing may have been a particularly prominent aspect of the life of some of the churches of Northern Egypt. This prayer may be compared with *AC*, 8.7, a prayer after the prayer for the catechumens but focusing upon energumens (those thought to be affected by evil spirits) rather than the sick in general. In *AC*, 8, 7 there is a prayer for energumens after the prayer for catechumens. The language of this prayer is very strong with four (aorist) imperatives (help, heal, rebuke and assist).

–help and heal]. 'help': Gk. *boēthein*—this term is used in the context of healings in papyrus texts (P. Lond VI. 1982, P. Oxy VIII.1161) and elsewhere.

–rebuke]. Lk. 4.39. Gk. *epitiman* is sometimes used in the Synoptic Gospels for exorcisms (see H. C. Kee, 'The Terminology of Mark's Exorcism Stories' in *NTS* 14 (1967/68) 232-246). Only Luke uses it of the incident of the healing of Peter's mother-in-law. Here it may reflect that illness is thought of as having a demonic cause (cf. N.17).

–give glory to your name]. Ps. 111.9.

[30] LAYING ON OF HANDS OF THE SICK

Lord God of mercies, stretch out your hand and grant that all the sick be healed. Grant them to be deemed worthy of health; deliver them from the sickness lying upon them. In the name of your only-begotten, let them be healed; let this holy name be to them a medicine for health and wholeness because through him to you be the glory and the power in holy Spirit both now and to all the ages of ages. Amen.

[23] PRAYER FOR THE HARVEST

Creator of heaven and earth, who has crowned the heaven through the chorus of the stars and through the radiance of the heavenly bodies, who has honoured

---

[30]: The prayer was presumably used in conjunction with the previous one and both Wordsworth (*BSPB*, p.37) and Cuming ('Thmuis Revisited', pp.569-570) indicate this, even though in the order of prayers in the MS, it is located together with the other prayers for laying on of hands. Cuming ('Thmuis Revisited', p.570) suggests this prayer may be a later addition (noticing an alteration in the vocabulary) and would more consistently have been placed in the MS prior to the laying on of hands of the people (N.29). The prayer is discussed in detail in *CHANT*, pp.306-312). Whereas in Ns.28 and 29 the central emphasis is on blessing and the terms *eulogia* and *eulogein* are used, they are not used in N.30. Here the emphasis is entirely upon health and healing. The prayer also begins in a more direct way than Ns. 28 and 29. Those two prayers use the passive voice of God stretching out the divine hand; here the active is used.

–worthy of health]. This is an unusual expression in early Christian texts concerning this theme, though the emphasis is upon being deemed worthy of God's spiritual gifts in a more general way is common and reflected elsewhere in *SS* (Ns. 1, 14, 19, 21).

–in the name . . . let his holy name]. The name of Jesus was understood to be powerful and efficacious in relation to healing and exorcisms in the early church, cf. Justin, *Dialogue* 30.3; 2 *Apol.*, 6.6; Irenaeus, *Haer.*, II.32.4.

–medicine]. Gk. *pharmakon*. The term is used in several prayers (Ns. 5. and 17) and is here associated directly with the name of Jesus.

–health and wholeness]. Gk. *hygeia* and *holokteria*. These terms seem to imply that what is envisaged is a state of physical as well as spiritual/emotional well-being.

[23]: This prayer reflects the hopes of a community dependent upon agriculture and therefore rain for its livelihood and betrays a rich theology of creation. Its occurrence here in the liturgy is suggestive of a Christian community seeking to relate its faith to its wider social and physical environment. There are petititions for rain and for the rising of the river (Nile) in the Liturgy of St. Mark in both a pre-anaphoral prayer and the anaphora (Cuming, *LSM*, p.26; *LEW*, p.19) and in similar prayers in the Liturgy of the Coptic Jacobites (*LEW*, pp.159, 168). These two liturgies reflect a similarly positive theology of the creation (ibidem). In this prayer there is no petition for the rising of the river(s) and Wordsworth (*BSPB*, p.31) observes that Thmuis had an abundant supply of river water. See also the prayer for first-fruits in *AC*, 8.40 which has a slightly different emphasis.

the earth with its fruits for the use of humankind, who has freely given[1] to the race of those who have been formed by you, to enjoy from above the dawn and the light of the heavenly bodies and to be nourished from below by the fruits of the earth. We pray, grant the fullest and most productive rains. Cause the earth to also bear fruit and yield abundantly for the sake of your loving kindness[2] and generosity. Remember those who call upon you; honour your holy and only catholic Church and listen to our petitions and prayers and bless all the earth, through your only-begotten Jesus Christ, through whom to you be the glory and the power in holy Spirit both now and to all the ages of ages. Amen.

[24] PRAYER FOR THE CHURCH

Lord God of the ages, God of the rational spirits, God of pure souls and of all who sincerely and in purity call upon you, you who are revealed in h eaven and are known to those pure spirits, you who are praised in song on earth and dwell in the catholic Church, being ministered to by holy angels and pure souls, you who made also a living chorus out of heaven for glory and praise of the truth. Grant that this church may be a living and pure church; grant it to have divine powers and pure angelical ministers in order that it may be able to praise you in purity. We beseech you on behalf of all the people of this church; be reconciled to all; yield to all; grant to all forgiveness of sins. Grant them no longer to sin in anything but become a wall to them and nullify every temptation. Have mercy upon the men and women and children and reveal yourself to all and let the knowledge of yourself be written in their hearts, through your only-begotten Jesus Christ, through whom to you be the glory and the power in holy Spirit both now and to all the ages of ages. Amen.

---

[1] freely given . . . been formed]. Wordsworth emended the MS at this point from charē-samenos . . . pepalaiōmenōi to charisamenos peplasmenōi. This was accepted by Brightman ('Sacramentary', p.102) and Funk, (DECA, V.II, p.166).
[2] Gk. philanthrōpia.

–chorus of the stars]. Brightman ('Sacramentary', p.110) observes some parallels to this phrase in Philo, de mund. opif, 45; Athanasius, c. Arian. 2.19; AC, 8 and 12 and Liturgy of St. Mark (Cuming, LSM, p.52; LEW, p.137).
–your loving-kindness . . . generosity]. Tit. 3.4.
–holy and only catholic Church]. Cf. the similar phrase in the Liturgy of St. Mark (Cuming, LSM, p.22; LEW, pp.126, 150, 160, 165 and elsewhere).

[24]: The emphasis upon purity (Gk. katharos) in this prayer is striking—occuring seven times. Wordsworth (BSPB, pp.37-38) suggests that it reflects the preparation of the faithful for the ensuing parts of the liturgy and may have been associated with ablutions of some sort which, in Egypt, may have involved the congregation as well as the clergy. There is no mention of the Kiss of Peace in SS, but we know perhaps from the Didache 14, and certainly from Justin (1 Apol., 67), that it was a feature of the eucharist from an early period and was incorporated into the major rites including the Egyptian (Cuming, LSM, p.17 and see TSL, p.198). Wordsworth (BSPB, p.38) suggests that it may have followed ablutions after this prayer.

–Lord God of the ages]. Ecclus. 36.19.
–spirits . . . God of . . . souls]. Num. 16.22.
–written in their hearts]. Heb. 8.10.

We call upon you, the Saviour and Lord, the God of all flesh[1] and Lord of every spirit, you who are blessed and the supplier of every blessing. Sanctify this bishop and keep him beyond temptation and give to him wisdom and knowledge and cause him to prosper in his experiences of your ways.

We beseech you also on behalf of our fellow-presbyters; sanctify them; give them wisdom and knowledge and orthodox teaching. Cause them to be ambassadors of your holy teaching, correctly and blamelessly.

Sanctify the deacons also, that they may be pure in heart[2] and in body and that they may be able to minister with a pure conscience[3] and to attend to the holy body and the holy blood.

---

[1] Num. 16.22.
[2] Mt. 5.8.
[3] 1 Tim. 3.9; 2 Tim. 1.3.

---

[25]: Canon 19 of the the Council of Laodicea referred to the 'three prayers of the Faithful' and these are generally found in Egyptian liturgies (as in the Liturgy of St. Mark, (Cuming, *LSM*, pp.15-16; *LEW*, p.121)) and involved prayers for peace, the bishop and clergy and the safe assembly of the congregations. See further Cuming, *LSM*, pp.99-101. *SS* does not have the first and third but Wordsworth (*BSBP*, p.38) believes the current prayer corresponds to the second of these.

This prayer, as in similar prayers, is in the form of a litany and there may have been responses between the petitions. It also illustrates the various orders of ministry. The term 'Sanctify' is only used in relation to the bishop, fellow presbyters and deacons who would have been formally ordained whereas the minor orders in the West and in Egypt were not (cf. *AT*, 11-14 and *CH*, 7, 9) in this period. The orders of ministry are somewhat less developed here than in Rome and Syria. Pope Cornelius refers in a letter in c.250 AD to sub-deacons, acolytes, exorcists, readers and doorkeepers in addition to the major orders (cited in Eusebius, *HE* VI 43.11). *AC* refers to deaconesses, sub-deacons and readers, who are ordained and confessors, virgins, widows and exorcists who are not (*AC*, 8, 19-26). See further notes to Ns. 12-14 below.

-give wisdom and knowledge]. This petition is offered for bishop and presbyters, presumably in the light of their organizational role and teaching function. In *CH*, 23 (unparalleled in *AT*) considerable emphasis in placed on the acquisition of knowledge by the faithful generally, 'we are to be zealous in pursuing knowledge in every way' (Bradshaw, *CH*, p.27).

-this bishop]. This statement clearly implies that the prayer was not said by the bishop. Wordsworth (*BSPB*, p.24) suggests a second celebrant or concelebrant is the explanation.

-fellow presbyters]. Brightman ('Sacramentary', p.110, n.27) suggests this may imply either the existence of a college of presbyters or alternatively, that a presbyter rather than a bishop, is reciting the prayer.

-deacons . . . pure]. Stress is placed on the purity of deacons in view of their role attending the eucharistic elements.

And we beseech you on behalf of the sub-deacons and readers and interpreters. Give rest to all the ministers[1] of the Church and grant to all mercy and compassion and improvement.

We pray for the monks and virgins; let them complete their course[2] blamelessly and their mode of life unfailingly, that they may be able to remain in purity and holiness all their days.

Have mercy also upon all who are married, husbands, wives and children and give to all a blessing of progress and improvement in order that all may beocme a living and chosen people, through your only-begotten Jesus Christ, through whom to you be the glory and the power in holy Spirit both now and to the ages of ages. Amen.

[26] PRAYER OF BENDING THE KNEE[1]

Father of the only-begotten, good and compassionate, merciful and loving of humanity and loving of souls, benefactor of all those who turn to you, receive

---

[1] Gk. *leitourgoi* is added by Brightman and Funk following Wobbermin.

[2] 2 Tim. 4.7.

[3] Gk. *gonuklisia*.

–interpreters]. Gk. *hermēneutēs*. Reflects a bilingual community where Coptic would have been the mother tongue for most in rural communities.

–improvement]. Gk. *prokoē*. It is difficult to grasp the exact sense of the use of this term which is used in a number of the prayers and again here in the petition for the Church. The emphasis seems to be on moral and spiritual progress, s.v. Lampe, *PGL*.

–monks and virgins]. The terms reflect the development of the ascetic movement which was very strong in Egypt and Sarapion himself was a monk (s.v. Serapion, *ODCC*) and close friend of Antony.

–virgins]. Wordsworth follows the very unlikely reading of the MS by Wobbermin at this point, see Brightman's note, 'Sacramentary', p.111, n.37.

–to the ages of ages]. One of two prayers in which 'all' is omitted in the doxology.

[26]: This prayer has no parallel in the Liturgy of St. Mark (Cuming, *LSM*, p.100) and no very satisfactory explanation has been offered for it. Wordsworth (*BSPB*, p.38) observes that the fact that Canon 20 of Nicaea forbade kneeling on Sundays and festivals creates some difficulty, as does the fact that it has little real parallel with either the prayer connected with kneeling in *AC*, 8 and 9 or the prayer of the veil in the Liturgy of the Coptic Jacobites. Wordsworth (*BSPB*, p.38) draws attention to the emphasis upon confession of sin and suggests that it may best be seen, along with N.27, as representing a confessional prayer, prior to the offertory. See further Brightman, 'Sacramentary', p.111, n.1.9).

–compassionate and merciful]. Ps. 85.15.

–loving of humanity]. Gk. *philanthrōpos*. This is a common term in the prayers and in Egyptian liturgies generally (*BSPB*, p.27), underlining along with other terms such as 'lover of souls' (*philopsychos* Wisd. of Solomon 11.26), the emphasis upon God's nature as loving.

humanity and loving of souls, benefactor of all those who turn to you, receive this petition and give to us knowledge and faith and godliness and holiness. Bring to nothing every passion, every evil pleasure, every sin from this people. Make them all become pure. Excuse the offences of all. For before you, the uncreated Father, through the only-begotten we kneel. Give to us a holy mind and full assistance. Give to us to seek you and love you; give to us to search and seek our your divine teachings.[1] Give to us your hand, Master, and raise us up. God of mercies, raises us up and make us look up to you. Uncover our eyes, grant to us boldness[2]; may you not allow us to be disgraced, nor to be ashamed, nor to condemn ourselves. Remove the bond that is against us. Write our names in the book of life; number us together with your holy prophets and apostles, through your only-begotten Jesus Christ, through whom to you be the glory and the power in holy Spirit now and to all the ages of ages. Amen.

[1] PRAYER OF OFFERING OF BISHOP SARAPION
It is fitting and right to praise, to hymn and to glorify you, the uncreated Father of the only-begotten Jesus Christ. We praise you, uncreated God, unsearchable, inexpressible and incomprehensible to all created existence.

---

[1] Gk. *ta logia.*
[2] Gk. *parrēsia.*

–give us your hand, Master . . . uncover our eyes]. The imagery here is quite powerful and may have also involved the ritual action of standing at this point.
–the bond that is against]. Col. 2.14.
–write our names . . . of life]. Phil. 4.3; Rev. 13.8.
–holy prophets and apostles]. Eph. 3.5. There is no direct reference to saints in the prayers.

[NB: The Introductory Note to N.1 follows on page 24 overleaf.]
–Title]. Other than the general title (see N.15) this is the only point at which the name of Bishop Sarapion occurs. If we are correct in thinking Sarapion was responsible for the final collection of prayers, it is very reasonable to assume that this was the anaphoral prayer used by Sarapion at Thmuis.
–it is fitting]. An introductory dialogue is probably to be assumed before the beginning of the preface. The flow of ideas in the Preface is rather different from the Liturgy of St. Mark which focuses more on creation and offering 'of this reasonable and bloodless service' (see *PTE*, p.48). The theme of God being known and making himself known through Christ is prominent in *SS*.

We praise you who are known by the Son, the only-begotten, the one through whom you have been spoken of, interpreted and made known to created nature. We praise you who knows the Son and reveals to the saints the glories concerning him; you who are known by your begotten Word and are seen by, and

---

[1]: The anaphora of SS has both significant parallels with, and differences from, other Egyptian liturgies including that of St. Mark, many of which are summarized by Yarnold in TSL, pp.237-239. Cuming (LSM, p.xxxvii) observes that in comparison with the Liturgy of St. Mark and the Deir Balyzeh Papyrus (see PTE, pp.45-46), SS often provides the earliest evidence and its anaphora is therefore of very considerable liturgical importance. H. Lietzmann in his classical study of 1926, Messe und Herrenmahl (ET: Mass and the Lord's Supper [Brill, 1979]) saw the anaphora of SS as providing one of the two basic eucharistic prototypes which went back to the Didache and the primitive Jerusalem liturgy, a theory that has not won wide support (see B. Capelle, 'L' Anaphore de Sérapion', in Le Museon 59 [1946] 425-443). In the Liturgy of St. Mark, the basic elements of the anaphora, in order, are: Preliminaries, Preface, Intercessions, Pre-Sanctus and Sanctus, Post-Sanctus (and first epiclesis?), Institution narrative, Second epiclesis and Doxology (see Cuming, LSM, pp.20-48). The anaphora of the SS is shorter and more simplified consisting of: Preface, Pre-Sanctus and Sanctus, Post Sanctus (and first epiclesis?), Institution narrative (with no anamnesis), Epiclesis of the Word, Prayers for the departed and recitation of the diptychs and an 'embryonic intercession' (Cuming, LSM, p.xxiv) and Doxology. Among the important differences in the SS are (1) the lack of mention of any preliminary dialogue (as generally in SS—perhaps because they were known by rote [see LSL, p.237])—note though that this dialogue, slightly modified, is virtually all that is retained in CH, 3 of AT's eucharistic prayer (see further Cuming, 'The Eucharist' in Essays on Hippolytus, ed. G. J. Cuming [Grove Books, 1978], p.43; (2) the prayers for the departed and reading of the diptychs and embryonic intercessions after the institution narrative which are seen by Cuming (LSM, pp.xxiii-xxvii) as the beginnings of a change from having the intercessions before the anaphora as they are in most liturgies to placing them in what he sees as the more primitive position reflected in the Strasbourg Papyrus, at the end of the anaphora (see further Cuming, LSM, pp.131-135 who takes issue with H. Engberding in his, 'Das anaphorische Fuebittgebet der griechischen Markusliturgie', Orientalia Christiana Periodica 30 [1964] 398-446), (3) the lack of an anamnesis which is a strong feature of Roman and Syrian liturgies, typically employing the term 'remembering' (cf. AT, 4 and AC, 8.12), whereas the Liturgy of St. Mark and other Egyptian rites use the term 'proclaiming' from 1 Cor. 11.26 [see LSM, pp.43-44, 124-125 and Cuming, 'The Eucharist', p.47]; (4) the epiclesis of the Word rather than of the Spirit (which Brightman ['Sacramentary', p.97] suggested in 1899 was probably unique though it is now clear that the more primitive view was not to make so clear a distinction between Word and Spirit (see further D. B. Capelle, 'L'Anaphora de Sérapion', Le Museon 59 (1946) 425-443; G. Dix, 'The Origins of the Epiclesis', in Theology 28 (1934) 125-37; 187-202 and Cuming, 'The Eucharist', pp.48-50). There is an English translation of the anaphora of St. Mark based on the Rossano MS in PTE, pp.48-55.

–are known . . . knows the Son and reveals]. Lk. 10.22; Mt. 9.27; 16.17.

revealed to the saints. We praise you, invisible Father, bestower of immortality. You are the source of life, the source of light, the source of all grace and all truth, lover of humanity and lover of the poor, you who are reconciled to all and draw all people to yourself through the coming of your beloved Son. We pray make us a living people. Give to us a spirit of light that we may know you the true God[1] and him whom you sent, Jesus Christ. Give us holy Spirit that we may be able to declare and explain your indescribable mysteries. Let the Lord Jesus and holy Spirit speak in us and let him praise you through us.

For you are far above every rule and authority and power and dominion and every name that is named, not only in this age but also in the age to come. Beside you stand thousands of thousands and ten thousand times ten thousand angels, archangels, thrones, dominions, principalities and authorities: beside you stand the two most honoured six winged seraphim with two wings covering the face, and with two the feet and with two flying and crying holy; with them accept also our acclamation of holiness as we say

Holy, holy, holy Lord Sabaoth,
Heaven and earth are full of your glory
Full is heaven, full also is the earth of your magnificent glory, Lord of hosts. Fill

---

[1] 'Theos' supplied.

-source of life]. Jer. 2.13.
-grace and all truth]. Jn. 1.14.
-draw all people]. Jn. 12.32.
-that we may know you . . . Jesus Christ]. Jn. 17.3.
-For you are far above]. These words introduce the pre-Sanctus and there is a very close identity in wording here with the Liturgy of St. Mark (Cuming, *LSM*, p.37; *LEW*, p.131) and the *Deir Balyzeh Papyrus* (*PTE*, p.45). See further Rodopolous, *The Sacramentary of Serapion*, pp.51-56 and Cuming, *LSM*, pp.119-120 who states that 'no early text of Mark includes the pre-Sanctus'.
-far above . . . age to come]. Ephes. 1.21 (the use of this verse is peculiar to Egypt, elsewhere Col. 1.16 is used [Cuming, *LSM*, p.120]).
-beside you stand . . . archangels]. Dan. 7.10.
-thrones, dominions . . . authorities]. Col. 1.16 (*SS*, unlike the Liturgy of St. Mark and *Deir Balyzeh*, includes both Eph. 1.21 and Col. 1.16).
-six winged seraphim . . . full of your glory]. Is. 6.2-3.
-Holy, holy, holy]. The sanctus seems to have been introduced to Christian worship from the synagogue but was not an early feature of the liturgies; it was not introduced to Rome until c.450 (Cuming, *LSM*, p.119). It is found in the Liturgy of St. Mark, *Deir Balyzeh*, evidently in the Louvain Coptic Fragment (*PTE*, p.46) and in other liturgies including *AC*, 8.27 and Theodore's *Catechical Homilies* (16.6).
-Full is heaven . . . your magnificent glory]. Introduces the words of the post-sanctus in similar works as are found in the Liturgy of St. Mark (Cuming, p.39; *LEW*, p.132), *Deir Balyzeh*, *Louvain Coptic Papyrus* and the *British Museum Tablet* (*PTE*, pp.45, 46, 44 respectively). See further Cuming, *LSM*, pp.120-122.
-full of your magnificent glory]. 2 Pet. 1.17.
-Lord of hosts]. Ps. 83.1.
-fill also this sacrifice]. In the Liturgy of St. Mark and the *British Museum Tablet* this petition reads 'Fill also this sacrifice with your blessing' (in *Deir Balyzeh* 'your glory'). See further *LSL*, p.199 and Cuming, *LSM*, pp.121-122.

also this sacrifice with your power and your participation for to you we have offered this living sacrifice, this bloodless offering.

To you we have offered this bread, the likeness of the body of the only-begotten. This bread is a likeness of the holy body, for the Lord Jesus Christ on the night in which he was betrayed took bread and brok it[1] and gave it to his disciples saying, 'Take and eat; this is my body which is broken for you for the forgiveness of sins.' Therefore we also making the likeness of the death, have offered the bread and we beseech you through this sacrifice, be reconciled to us all and be merciful, God of truth. And as this bread was scattered over the mountains and was gathered together and became one loaf[2], so also gather together your holy Church from every nation and every region and every city and village and house and make one living catholic Church.

---

[1] 'It' supplied.
[2] Gk. simply *'eis hen'*.

–we have offered]. Gk. *prosēnegkamen*. The use of the perfect here in SS's offering prayer has led to considerable debate. See H. Leitzmann, *Mass and the Lord's Supper*, pp.152-160; A. D. Nock, 'The Anaphora of Serapion', *JTS* 30 (1928-9) 381-390. E. Yarnold (*TSL*, p.238) suggests that the words imply that the act of offering is regarded as being already completed prior to the eucharistic prayer.

–living sacrifice]. Rom. 12.1.

–living sacrifices ... bloodless offering]. Reflects the shift in ideas from an original (Pauline) offering of the self to an offering of the eucharistic gifts (see Cuming, *LSM*, pp.107-108 and G. Dix, *The Shape of the Liturgy*, pp.166-167).

–we have offered ... bread]. This leads in the Institution narrative of SS with its distinctive use of the term 'likeness' (*homoiōma*) and the breaking up of the narrative with reference to the 'corn prayer' taken form the *Didache* (see below).

–for the Lord Jesus Christ ... broken for you]. 1 Cor. 12.23, 24; Mk. 6.6; Lk. 22.19; Mt. 26.26. Egyptian liturgies typically introduce the Institution with a causal particle (*hoti* or *gar*) which implies that the narrative provides the justification of the eucharistic celebration (see A. D. Nock, 'The Anaphora of Serapion' in *JTS* 30 (1929) 386 and Cuming, *LSM*, pp.122-123).

–the likeness of the death]. Ro. 6.5.

–God of truth]. Ps. 30.6.

–And as this bread ... became one loaf]. This saying which also appears in the same place in *Deir Balyzeh* and apparently comes from the *Didache* 9, is the focus of a petition, unique amongst the liturgies for the gathering together and unifying of the church (see Yarnold, *TSL*, p.238). It should also be observed that SS has no command to 'do this in remembrance'.

And we have also offered the cup, the likeness of the blood, for the Lord Jesus Christ took a cup after the supper and siad to his disciples. 'Take and[1] drink; this is the new covenant which is my blood, poured out for you for the forgiveness of sins.' Therefore we have also offered the cup, presenting a likeness of the[2] blood.

God of truth, let your holy Word come upon this bread that the bread may become body of the Word, and upon this cup, that the cup may become blood of the Truth. And make all those who share it receive a medicine of life for the healing of every sickness and for a strengthening of all advancement[3] and virtue, not for condemnation, God of truth, nor for reproof or reproach.

For we have called upon you, the uncreated, through the only-begotten, in holy Spirit. Let this people have mercy; let them by it be deemed worthy of advancement; let angels be sent as helpers for the people for an abolition of the evil One and for a strengthening of the Church.

And we beseech you also on behalf of all those who have been laid to rest, whose commemoration we make:

---

[1] 'and' supplied.
[2] 'the' supplied.
[3] Gk. *prokopē*.

–for the Lord Jesus . . . took a cup . . . for forgiveness of sins]. 1 Cor. 12.23-25; Mt. 26.27-28; Lk. 22.20.

–likeness]. Gk. *homoiōma*—now used twice in relation to the blood.

–God of truth]. Ps. 30.6.

–let your holy Word come upon]. SS is unique amongst the liturgies in the focus on the Word rather than the Spirit in this epiclesis. It is no longer at all clear that this reflects an unorthodox understanding of the Spirit (cf. Botte, 'L'Eucologe de Sérapion est-il authentique?' in *Oriens Christianus* 48 (1964) 50.57) in view of the intimate association of Word and Spirit in Christian thought prior to the debates of the mid to later fourth century (see Cuming, 'Thmuis Revisited', pp.572-575; *LSM*, pp.xxxvi-xxxvii and Yarnold, *TSL*, p.239).

–come upon]. Gk: *epidēmēsai*. This term is normally used in relation to the incarnation or occasionally the coming of the Spirit and is unexpected in the context of an epiclesis, see Brightman, 'Sacramentary', p.97. The fundamental sense of the term is 'to be at home', 'to stay in a place', s.v. Lampe, *PGL*.

–a medicine of life for . . . healing]. This focus upon healing in an epiclesis seems to be unique to SS and reflects the significant interest of the author/compiler of the prayer in the theme of illness and healing (see above note on Ns. 27, 22). The eucharistic elements are seen as health giving as well as strengthening for the Christian life. Brightman ('Sacramentary', p.112) suggests the phrase 'medicine of lilfe' may have a parallel in Ignatius, *Ephes.* 20 'one bread . . . which is a medicine of immortality'.

–God of truth]. Ps. 30.6.

–For we have called . . .]. This petition begins a brief section of prayers which initially focuses upon the faithful and the Church.

–those laid to rest]. The intercession here for the departed and the ensuing reading of the diptychs here rather than during the Preface is unique among the Egyptian liturgies (Yarnold, *TSL*, p.239).

After the Recitation of the names.
Sanctify these souls, for you know them all. Sanctify all those who have been laid to rest in the Lord and number them with all your holy powers and give them a place and an abode in your kingdom.

Receive also the thanksgiving of the people and bless those who have offered the offerings and the eucharistic elements and grant health and wholeness, contentment and all advancement of soul and body to this whole people, through your only-begotten Jesus Christ in holy Spirit; as it was and is and will be for generation upon generations and to all the ages of ages. Amen.

[2] AFTER THE PRAYER THE FRACTION AND A PRAYER AT THE FRACTION
Deem us worthy of this communion[1] also, God of truth and make our bodies contain purity and our souls contain prudence and knowledge, and make us

---

[1] Gk. *koinōnia.*

−*Recitation of the names*]. The names of the dead and in some cases those who had made offerings were inscribed on wooden tablets which were read out in the liturgy (see *LEW*, pp.574-575 s.v. diptychs). It is well illustrated in the *Strasbourg Papyrus (PTE*, p.43).
−*Sanctify these souls*]. The intercessor concludes with prayer for the sanctification of those remembered.
−*in the Lord*]. Rv. 14.13.
−*Receive also the thanksgiving*]. This petition brings the anaphora to a conclusion with a particular emphasis on those who have offered the offerings and the eucharistic elements, on health and wholeness and spiritual progress for the whole people. Wordsworth (*BSPB*, pp.45-46) suggested the offerings include the bread and wine for communion and gifts for an agapé or for the sick.
−*through your only-begotten in holy Spirit*]. Cuming (*LSM*, p.129) suggests this may be the original Egyptian formula of the doxology.
−*as it was and is and will be for*]. Concluding doxology which Brightman ('Sacramentary', p.107) took to be a response by the people since it appears in identical form as a response at the end of the anaphora of St. Mark in *LEW*, p.135 and other Egyptian liturgies (cf. *LEW*, pp.180, 190, 233) though the actual text of St. Mark abbreviates the phrase with simply the words 'as it was and is' (Cuming, *LSM*, p.48 and *LEW*, p.134).

[2]: The title of this prayer is also rubrical in nature. It is not clear what 'After the prayer' means; does it mean the anaphora or the Lord's prayer? Wordsworth (*BSPB*, p.65) thought it may be the latter as it is not otherwise referred to in the prayers. Cuming (*TLM*, p.142) thinks it probably means the anaphora. We do know however that the Lord's prayer was included in Egyptian liturgies at an early stage (Yarnold, *TSL*, p.239). In the Liturgy of St. Mark (Cuming, *LSM*, p.50) it comes after the doxology.

[continued on p.29 opposite]

−*Deem us worthy*]. This expression is found in N.30 (see note) in relation to health—here it is used in relation to the communion.
−*bodies . . . souls*]. See note above, N.29.

wise, O God of mercies, through the partaking of the body and the blood, for through the only-begotten be to you the glory and the power in holy Spirit now and to all the ages of ages. Amen.

[3] LAYING ON OF HANDS OF THE PEOPLE AFTER DISTRIBUTION OF THE BROKEN BREAD TO THE CLERGY

I stretch out my hand upon this people and I pray that your hand of truth may be stretched out and a blessing given to this people because of your loving kindness[1], O God of mercies and the mysteries[2] that are present. Let your hand of reverence and of power and of self-discipline[3] and of purity and of all holiness bless this people and maintain it for progress[4] and improvement, through your only-begotten Jesus Christ in holy Spirit now and to all the ages of ages. Amen.

[1] Gk. *philanthrōpia.*
[2] Gk. *ta mystēria.*
[3] Gk. *sōphronismos.*
[4] Gk. *prokopē.*

[2—continued]: The fraction was a more important part of the liturgy in Egypt and Syria than the West (see Cuming, *LSM*, pp.55, 141-142; *LEW*, p.136). It is often omitted in references to the liturgy by Western writers and is not referred to in *AC* or *TD* though it is (briefly) by Chrysostom (see in *LEW*, pp.478 and 480, n.29) and by Theodore of Mospuestia (*Catechetical Homilies*, 16.15-20, see *TSL*, pp.233, 235, 239) and further Brightman, 'Sacramentary', p.97. This particular prayer however is not paralleled in the fraction in the Liturgy of St. Mark (Cuming, *LSM*, p.55 and see *ibid.*, pp.141-142; *LEW*, p.136). In the Liturgy of the Coptic Jacobites there is a very long prayer at the fraction which is followed by the Lord's prayer (*LEW*, pp.181-182). But our prayer here is similar in length and content to the prayer in the Liturgy of the Abyssinian Jacobites (*LEW*, p.234).

–partaking]. Gk. *metalēpsis*
–God of truth]. Ps. 30.6.

[3]: It seems from the rubrical title of this prayer that after the conclusion of N.2, the clergy were communicated and this was then followed by another prayer of blessing of the people before they communicated. Wordsworth refers to this prayer as 'the Inclination' which was a prayer of blessing delivered while the people had their heads bowed. A prayer of inclination is also found in the Liturgy of St. Mark (Cuming, *LSM*, pp.52, 139; *LEW*, pp.136-137) and in the Liturgy of the Coptic Jacobites (*LEW*, p.183) and the Egyptian Liturgy of St. Basil (*LEW*, p.411).

–I stretch out . . . I pray]. There is a change to the first person here, cf. N.28, 'We stretch out . . . we pray'.
–the mysteries]. Clearly means the eucharistic elements.
–my hand . . . your hand]. The contrast underlines the fact that the ritual act of the celebrant is thought to be evocative of God reaching to convey a blessing on the people.
–self discipline . . . purity . . . holiness]. The blessing seems to be intended to help prepare the people to be able to receive the communion worthily.

Translation   29

[4] PRAYER AFTER THE DISTRIBUTION TO THE PEOPLE
We give thanks to you, Master, because you have called those who have erred[1] and you have won over[2] those who have sinned and you have removed the threat[3] that was against us, making allowance for us by your loving kindness[4] and wiping it away by repentance and excluding it by the knowledge concerning yourself. We give thanks to you that you have given to us a sharing of body and blood. Bless us, bless this people, enable us to have a share with the body and the blood, through your only-begotten Son through whom to you be the glory and the power in holy Spirit to all the ages of ages. Amen.

[5] PRAYER FOR THE OILS AND WATERS THAT ARE OFFERED
We bless these created things[5] through the name of your only-begotten Jesus

[1] Gk. *esphalmenoi*.
[2] Gk. *prospoiēsasthai*.
[3] Gk. *apeilē*.
[4] Gk. *philanthrōpia*.
[5] Gk. *ta ktismata* (emended from *ktisma*).

[4]: This prayer forms a post-communion thanksgiving prayer but it is significantly different from that in the Liturgy of St. Mark (Cuming, *LSM*, p.58 and see pp.143-144). Cuming (*LSM*, p.144) notes that there was also a thanksgiving prayer at Jerusalem in Cyril's time and in Chrysostom's Antioch (cf. *LEW*, pp.186, 192, 242). The initial focus in the prayer is on redemption with thanksgiving for the eucharist following.

–the threat]. Presumably the threat of judgement is meant.
–knowledge]. Here knowledge of salvation.
–sharing of body and blood]. 1 Cor. 10.16.
–bless]. The final emphasis of the prayer shifts to the blessing of the people.

[5]: The more usual position for such a prayer is after the words of Institution and this is illustrated by prayers in *TD*, 24 (Cooper and Maclean, *TTL*, pp.77-78) and in the anaphora of the Ethiopic Church Ordinances (*LEW*, p.190), a prayer which itself has close parallels to the prayer 'Of the Offering of oil' in *AT* 5. This latter prayer also appears to be in close proximity to the words of Institution in that 'rite' and is followed by another prayer for the offering of cheese and olives. These prayer are carried over a simplified form in the episcopal ordination liturgy in *CH*, 3.
   In this prayer the emphasis is entirely upon the blessing of offered oil and water that they might be efficacious in bringing physical health and freedom from any demonic power. The practice was apparently that lay people would bring oil and water to be offered for blessing and taken home for private use, see further *CHANT*, pp.279-298; Brightman, 'Sacramentary', pp.260-261 and C. Harris, 'Visitation of the Sick, Unction, Imposition of the Hands and Exorcism' in *Liturgy and Worship*, (ed. W. Lowther Clark and C. Harris) (SPCK, London, 1932), pp.501-505. It is likely that the clergy in their ministrations to the sick might also require at least oil. There are prayers that closely parallel this prayer in *AC*, 8.29 and *TD*, 1.24 (*TTL*, p.78) involving prayer over offered water and oil. This prayer is discussed in detail in *CHANT*, pp.297-303.

Christ, we name the name of him who suffered, who was crucified and rose again and is seated at the right hand of the uncreated, upon this water and this oil. Grant healing power upon these created things[1], so that every fever and every demon and every illness may be cured[2] through the drinking and the anointing, and may the partaking of these created things be a healing medicine[3] and a medicine[3] of wholeness[4] in the name of your only-begotten Jesus Christ, through whom to you be the glory and the power in holy Spirit to all the ages of ages. Amen.

[6] LAYING ON OF HANDS AFTER THE BLESSING OF THE WATER AND THE OIL
Loving God[5] of truth, let the communion[6] of the body and of the blood remain with this people. Let their bodies be living bodies and their souls be pure[7] souls.

---

[1] Gk. *ta ktismata* (emended from *ktisma*).
[2] Gk. *appalagēnai*.
[3] Gk. *pharmakon*.
[4] Gk. *holoklēria*.
[5] Gk. *philanthrōpos*.
[6] Gk. *koinōnia*.
[7] Gk. *katharos*.

-we name the name]. The name of Jesus is often emphasized in prayer for healing (see *CHANT*, pp.143, 159, passim.). Jesus is sometimes described as a physician in early Christian writers, see further *CHANT*. p.290, n.75).
-Grant healing power upon]. The understanding appears to be that the elements themselves will become bearers of the healing power of Christ, see *CHANT*, p.300. The adjective 'healing' (*therapeutikos*) is rare in Christian writers and may indicate the author/compiler had an extensive vocabulary concerned with illness and healing at his disposal (*ibid.*, p.301).
-every fever ... every illness]. Cf. P. Turner 49 (lines 9-12) in *Papyri Greek and Egyptian* (Egypt Exploration Society, London, 1981), pp.192-193.
-healing medicine]. Cf. N.30, 'medicine for health ....'
-medicine of wholeness]. Gk. *pharmakon holoklērias*. Cf. 'medicine for ... wholeness' in N.30. This seems to reflect a concern for h ealth in a comprehensive sense—cf. Ns. 30 and 17.

[6]: This prayer may have been a final Benediction (so Wordsworth, *BSPB*, p.42). Certainly the communion is in mind and it is clear that it has already been celebrated. The interest of the prayer seems to be on the hope that the significance and effect of having celebrated the Eucharist and shared the 'communion of the body and ... blood' remain with the participants. In this respect the emphasis of this prayer is different from the final blessing of other Egyptian liturgies (cf. Liturgy of St. Mark, Cuming, *LSM*, pp.59-60; *LEW*, p.142; Liturgy of Coptic Jacobites, *LEW*, p.187; Egyptian Church Ordinances, p.192). This prayer would conclude the eucharistic liturgy and be followed by the dismissal (see Yarnold, *TSL*, p.239).

-God of truth]. Ps. 30.6.
-communion of the body and the blood]. 1 Cor. 10.16-17.

Give this blessing as a preservation of their[1] communion and a confirmation[2] of the eucharist[3] that has taken place and deem blessed all of them in common and make them elect, through your only-begotten Jesus Christ in holy Spirit both now and to all the ages of ages. Amen.

[7] SANCTIFICATION[4] OF WATERS

King and Lord of everything and Maker of the whole world[5], who has freely granted salvation to all created nature through the descent of your only-begotten Jesus Christ, who redeemed the human race[6] which was created by yourself through the coming[7] of your ineffable Word. Watch[8] now from heaven and look

---

[1] Gk. 'the'.
[2] Gk. *asphalia*.
[3] Gk. *eucharistia*.
[4] Gk. *hagiasmos*.
[5] Gk. *tōn holon*.
[6] Gk. *to plasma*.
[7] Gk. *epidemia*.
[8] The form here is *ephide* which Cuming [*LSM*, p.128] suggests is an Egyptian spelling for *epide* (verb: *eporan* or *ephoran*).

–confirmation of ... eucharist]. It is difficult to be certain what is meant here. The term *asphleia* is not used in Lampe, *PGL* though it is a NT word (Lk. 1.4; 1 Thess. 5.23). It is used in the papyri with a technical legal sense of 'bond, security' (*BAGD*, s.v.) and Wordsworth (*BSPB*, p.67) renders it this way. I take it more in the sense of 'assurance, certainty' (*LSJ*, s.v.) and hence a confirming of the Eucharist. The petition is them that the blessing may confirm the benefits experienced in the liturgy and the sharing of bread and wine.

[7]: Prayers 7.11 follow in order in the MS and all relate to baptismal practices. So do Ns. 15 and 16 Cuming ('Thmuis Revisited', pp.569-570) groups them separately at the beginning of the document with a collection of 'Preliminary blessing of oils'. These prayers add to our knowledge of early baptismal rites and were published by E. C. Whitaker, *Documents of Baptismal Liturgy* (SPCK, London, 2nd ed., 1970). The *Didache* 7 and *AT*, 21 prefer running water for baptism but it is not seen as essential. It has been suggested that the use of still water as against running water contributed to the sense of need for a prayer of sanctification over the baptismal water (see J. D. C. Fisher, 'The Consecration of Water in the Early Rite of Baptism', in *Studia Patristica 2* [1957] 41-46) and the earliest evidence for this is found in Tertullian (see Whitaker, *Documents*, pp.7-10). *AT*, 21 states 'first let prayer be made over the water' (Cuming, *Hippolytus*, p.18) and *CH*, 19 speaks of 'water, running and pure, prepared and sanctified' (Bradshaw, *The Canons*, p.22). SS's prayer of sanctification of water is clearly much more developed and is particularly noteworthy for the epiclesis of the Spirit and the Word.

–human race]. This term (*to plasma*) could be variously rendered—but the link with redemption suggests it is probably humankind that is in view.
–Watch now ... look upon]. Ps. 79.15.

upon these waters and fill them with holy Spirit. Let your ineffable Word be in them and transform their energy and prepare the waters, being filled with your grace to be productive in order that the mystery[1] which is now being celebrated may not be found to be without effect in those who are being regenerated, but may fill them all divine grace as they go down and are baptized. Loving[2] Benefactor, spare your own Creation, save what has been created by your right hand, and form all who are being regenerated to your divine and ineffable form in order that, through having been formed and regenerated, they may be able to be saved and be deemed worthy of your kingdom. And as your only-begotten Word came down upon the waters of the Jordan and rendered them holy, so now also let him come down[3] on these waters and make them holy and spiritual in order that those being baptized may be no longer flesh and blood but spiritual and be able to worship you, the uncreated Father, through Jesus Christ in holy Spirit, through whom to you be the glory and the power in holy Spirit now and to all the ages of ages. Amen.

---

[1] Gk. *mystērion.*
[2] Gk. *philanthrōpos.*
[3] Gk. *katerchesthai.*

–these waters]. The import of the plural is unclear but it could imply flowing water piped into a baptistry tank (see J. G. Davies, *The Architectural Setting of Baptism* (London, 1962), pp.25f).
–fill them with holy Spirit]. An initial invocation of the Spirit to embue the water.
–your . . . Word be in them]. This statement, coming straight after the invocation, implies a very close identity of Word and Spirit, consistent with the later second invocation, of the Word (see below).
–transform their energy . . . your grace]. The thought of the invocation is continued with a very explicit petition for the Word to bring about a change in the waters (Gk. *metapoiein*).
–the mystery . . . being celebrated]. The rite of baptism. It is used again in this sense in N.8. In N.3 *mystēria* is used of the eucharist and may be also in N.29.
–not without effect]. The adequate preparation of the water seems to be related to the effectiveness of any ensuing baptisms.
–are being regenerated]. This and the later references to regeneration (cf. Ns. 8, 15, 10, 11, 16) imply a close, though perhaps not complete, association of regeneration with baptism (cf. Tit. 3.5).
–they go down]. Into the water—presumably in a baptistry in a church. Immersion seems to be implied though Davies (*Architectural Setting*, pp.23-26) has shown that often baptistry baths were not deep enough for total immersion.
–deemed worthy of your kingdom]. 2 Thess. 1.5.
–Word . . . waters of the Jordan]. Presumably a reference to Jesus' baptism (see Brightman, 'Sacramentary', p.248). Cf. the Coptic Baptismal Rite where 'the Jordan' is an expression for the font (*DBL*, p.86).
–let him come down]. The second epiclesis, now of the Word. The thrust of the petition here is that the waters be made 'holy and spiritual'.
–no longer flesh . . . spiritual]. Reflects the theological understanding of the change from the old nature to the new.

[8] PRAYER FOR THOSE BEING BAPTIZED

We beseech you, God of truth, on behalf of this your servant and we pray that you may deem him worthy of the divine mystery and of your ineffable regeneration. For he is now offered to you, loving[1] God[2]; we set him apart for you. Grant him to participate[3] in this divine regeneration in order that he is no longer led by anyone perverse or evil but always serves[4] you and keeps your commandments, guiding him through your only-begotten Word, because through him to you be the glory and the power in holy Spirit both now and to the ages of ages. Amen.

---

[1] Gk. *philanthrōpos.*
[2] *'theos'* supplied.
[3] Gk. *koinōnēsai.*
[4] Gk. *latreuein.*

---

[8]: This prayer clearly concerns the preparation of the catechumens for baptism. Adults would normally have undergone a lengthy period of preparation, usually forty days (though *AT*, 17 speaks of three years) and concluded with examination, exorcism and fasting (the ancient practice in Alexandria was for a forty-day fast after Epiphany at the end of which time baptisms were conducted, see Bradshaw, *The Canons*, p.6). These procedures are not mentioned in *SS*. The final stage of baptism had different elements in different areas but usually involved final preparatory rites such as: entry into the baptistry, stripping, pre-baptismal anointing with oil of exorcism and the renunciation of the devil (see Yarnold, *TSL*, pp.134-136) and the last stage with adhesion to Christ, blessing of the baptismal water, immersion, post-baptismal anointing, redressing in white, various rites for the gift of the Spirit, often the giving of a lighted candle or lamp and the re-entry into the church and participation in the eucharist (see Yarnold, *LSL*, pp.136-141). Prayer N.8 of the *SS* would be used in the context of the final preparatory rites. Brightman ('Sacramentary', p.249) suggests that it may have had an exorcistic function in view of the words 'he is no longer led by anyone perverse or evil'. Exorcistic procedures and rites were however usually more explicit than this (cf. *AT*, 20 and 21 and *CH*, 19) and I think Brightman's observation is unlikely to be correct. The thrust of N.8 is on an offering and a setting apart of the catechumens to, and for, God as they prepare to undergo the ceremonies.

–God of truth]. Reflects the frequent emphasis in these prayers on being worthy of God's blessings (so N.7, N.2).
–deem him worthy]. A similar phrase occurs in N.7, alluding there to 2 Thess. 1.5.
–divine mystery]. Here again the rite of baptism, cf. n. N.7.
–regeneration]. A frequent term in *SS* in relation to baptism. It is used twice here and elsewhere (see n. N.7).
–in the holy Spirit]. This is the only doxology which includes a definite article with *hagion pneuma.* The vocabulary of this prayer generally is similar to the others in the collection and it is difficult to attach any special significance to the use of the article here.

[9] A PRAYER AFTER THE RENUNCIATION[1]

Almighty Lord, seal[2] the promise[3] of this your servant having now come to you and make him steadfast and protect his character and his way of life[4], in order that he may no longer serve evil ways[5] but may worship[6] the[7] God of truth and may serve you, the maker of all things, that he may be made perfect[8] and truly your own, through your only-begotten Jesus Christ, through whom be to you the glory and the power in holy Spirit now and to all the ages of ages. Amen.

[1] Gk. *apotagē*.
[2] Gk. *sphragisai*.
[3] Gk. *sygkatathesis*.
[4] Gk. *ēthos*.
[5] Gk. *tois cheirosin*.
[6] Gk. *latreuein*.
[7] 'the' is preceded by *en*. Brightman ('Sacramentary', p.270, n. 1.9) suggests reading *soi* or *en tō pneumati*.
[8] Gk. *teleion*.

---

[9]: The renunciation was a central feature of the ancient baptismal rites (cf. Tertull., *de Corona* 3; *AT*, 21, Cyril of Jerusalem, *Mystagogic Catecheses*, 1.4, *CH*, 19; see further on this subject H. A. Kelly, *The Devil at Baptism: Ritual Theology and Drama*, (Connell Univ. Press, Ithaca, 1985)). In the East the practice was to face west for the renunciation but then east for the act of adhesion (Cyril, *Myst. Cat.*, 1.4). This practice seems to have become widespread. It is not mentioned in *AT* but it is in *CH* (19) and this probably reflects general Egyptian practice by that time (see further E. Yarnold, *The Awe-Inspiring Rites of Initiation: Baptismal Homilies of the Fourth Century* (Slough, 1972), p.18). A prayer of this kind is not mentioned in *CH* (19) where the renunciation leads straight into anointing with the oil of exorcism, though it is difficult to be sure what is simply the practice of *AT* reflected in *CH* and when it is indicating local Alexandrian practice. Brightman ('Sacramentary', pp.269-270) has marshalled Egyptian Patristic evidence for the use of renunciation and confession of faith (note though his belief that *CH* was the source of *AT* (i.e. Egyptian Church Order).

–seal the promise]. This seems to state the import of the prayer—a prayer to confirm the rejection of Satan and all to do with him (cf. *CH*, 19 'I renounce you Satan, and all your service'). Brightman ('Sacramentary', p.270) notes *sygkatathesis* is not a technical ritual term, but is used in relation to baptism by Chrysostom (*hom. XL in 1 Cor. 1*). It is also used this way by Basil of Caesarea (*de Spiritu*, 28), see further Lampe, *PGL*. On the seal in baptism, see F. J. Dölger, *Sphragis* (Paderborn, 1911); G. Dix, *The Theology of Confirmation in Relation to Baptism* (Dacre, London, 1946); 'The Seal in the Second Century' in *Theology* 51 (1948), 7-12; J. E. L. Oulton, 'Second Century Teaching on Holy Baptism' in *Theology* 50 (1947) 86-91; G. W. H. Lampe, *The Seal of the Spirit* (SPCK, London, 2nd, edn. 1967).

–this your servant]. The phrase is also used in Ns. 8, 10, 11. Cf. similar expressions in Ns. 12, 13 14. The noun is *doulos*.

–steadfast . . . way of life]. It was imporotant for apologetic as well as personal reasons that a person being baptized was faithful in following the Christian lifestyle.

–evil ways]. It is difficult to know what is meant by *tois cheirosin*. Wordsworth (*BSPB*, p.70) reads 'those that are worse'. Brightman ('Sacramentary', p.270) suggested it may be an allusion to idolatrous practices in Egypt.

–the God of truth]. Wisd. of Solomon 11.26; Ps. 85.15.

–may worship . . . may serve you]. These terms imply the nature of the lifestyle to which the (new) Christian is called.

–made perfect]. Cf. Mt. 5.48.

PRAYERS[1] OF SARAPION, BISHOP OF THMUIS

[15] PRAYER FOR THE ANOINTING OF THOSE BEING BAPTIZED

Master, lover of humanity[2] and lover of souls[3], compassionate and merciful God[4] of truth, we call upon you, being convinced by, and obeying the promises

---

[1] Gk. *proseuch*, is abbreviated and could be singular or plural. I take it as the latter.
[2] Gk. *philanthrōpos*.
[3] Gk.*philopsychos*.
[4] Brightman/Funk supply *'theos'*.

[Title]: Neither Brightman nor Funk include this title in their text although the words do appear in the MS between Ns. 14 and 15 and Brightman prints them in this position in the list of titles ('Sacramentary', p.89) and refers to them later (*ibid.*, p.270, n.1.15). Cuming ('Thmuis Revisited', pp.569-570) has argued that this title is best seen as the title for the whole Sacramentary and N.15 therefore would be the first of the prayers in the collection, grouped with two further 'blessings of oil' (Ns. 16, 17). I have therefore inserted the title at this point though, on the basis of Cuming's argument, this really represents the beginning of the original MS.

[15]: How was this prayer used? Brightman ('Sacramentary', pp.264 and 251) took it to be a prayer said at the anointing of the catechumen with the oil of exorcism and he positioned it accordingly after N.9. Cuming ('Thmuis Revisited', pp.570-571) however, argued that while it can be seen this way, the two other prayers that follow in the MS (Ns. 16, 17) have a clearly consecratory nature and therefore this one must also. It is, in his view, a 'preliminary prayer'. Cuming may be correct in this but a difficulty with this view is the words 'we anoint with this anointing oil . . .' while N.16 says 'those who are anointed (*tois chriomenois*) with it' and N.17 similarly. One possibly might be that the prayer was indeed first in the original MS but placed there because it concerned oil, even though its use related to anointing during the baptism rite. It *is* difficult to be certain either way. The force of Cuming's point ('Thmuis Revisited', p.571) that other prayers used at the moment of baptism or ordination have a word such as *touton* or *tonde* perhaps tips the balance in Cuming's favour. It might in this case be beter to render *aleimma* in the title as 'anointing oil' and hence 'Prayer for the Anointing Oil . . .'. In both *AT*, 21 and *CH*, 19 the baptismal oils are blessed by the bishop during the rite, just prior to their actual use. In both, the 'oil of exorcism' is used after the renunciation and an 'oil of thanksgiving/anointing' after the immersion, Bradshaw (*The Canons*, p.22) has observed that in the ancient Egyptian tradition, the pre-baptismal anointing was not primarily exorcistic and he cites the evidence of *SS*, 15. It should however be noted that the prayer does speak of 'satanic effect' and 'attacks of the malevolent powers'. H. A. Kelly, *The Devil at Baptism*, (pp 138-139) interprets this language as 'apotropaic' rather than exorcistic in the full sense. This certainly points to the oil being for pre-baptismal anointing. *AC*, 42.3 (*DBL*, p.30) describes a prayer of blessing the oil for pre-baptismal anointing. See further on baptismal anointing G. Winkler, 'The Original Meaning of the Prebaptismal Anointing and its Implications' in *Worship* 52 (1978) 24-45. For the emphasis on healing in this prayer see *CHANT*, pp.313-315 (though I have modified my view on the purpose of the prayer).

–lover of souls]. Wisd. of Solomon 11.26.
–compassionate and merciful]. Ps. 85.16.

of your only-begotten who has said, 'if you forgive the sins of anyone, they are forgiven.' And we anoint with this anointing oil those (men) approaching[1] (or those women approaching) this divine regeneration, beseeching you that our Lord Christ Jesus may work a healing and strengthening power with it and reveal himself[2] through this anointing oil, and eradicate from their soul, body and spirit, every indication of sin and transgression or satanic effect, and by his own grace grant them forgiveness, that dying to sin, they will live for righteousness and being refashioned through this anointing and being cleansed through the washing and being renewed by the Spirit they will be fully able to overcome,

---

[1] The MS is somewhat unclear here and I follow Brightman/Funk and not Wobbermin (see note below).
[2] 'himself' supplied.

-if you forgive . . . are forgiven]. Jn. 20.23.
-those men approaching (or those women approaching]. The Greek of the MS (*tous prostasei prosiouas*) is difficult here but Wordsworth followed Wobbermin (*Altchristliche*, p.12) whose 'violent' emendation is most unlikely (*tous prosthesei prosiontas*). Brightman's suggestion (*tous prosiontas ē prosiousas*) is much more possible and is followed here on the basis of a somewhat similar alternative in N.18. The nouns 'men' and 'women' or something similar need to be supplied to bring out the male and female participles in Greek.
-this divine regeneration]. i.e. baptism.
-a healing and strengthening power]. This prayer also provides evidence of the interest in healing in *SS*. Here the emphasis may be on healing in a spiritual sense as well as a physical in view of the reference to soul, body and spirit. The term *iatikos* (healing) is a medical term used by Galen and Dioscurides and is very rare in Christian writers in a literal sense (*iatikos* occurs in *AC*, V.16.5 in the Funk edition but M. Metzger (*Les Constitutions apostoliques*, vol. 356 (Éditions du Cerf, Paris, 1987)), p.218 reads the variant *iamatikos*). The word is used again in N.17 (see *CHANT*, p.289). The petition is that the oil will become efficacious.
-eradicate]. This seems to imply an apotropaic effect from the use of oil and this is borne out by the reference to 'satanic effect' (see Kelly, *The Devil at Baptism*, pp.138-139).
-soul body and spirit]. This trichotomous formula is used again in N.17. It is used in 1 Thess. 5.23 and in Irenaeus, *Adv. Haer.*, V.6.1 and P.Oxy VIII.1161 (see further Brightman, 'Soul, Body, Spirit' in *JTS* 2 (1900/1901) 273-274 and *CHANT*, pp.30, 31-33, 295).
-dying to sin . . . righteousness]. 1 Pet. 2.24.
-refashioned through this anointing]. This is a further indication of the strong note of expectancy about the future effect of the oil.
-cleansed . . . the washing]. Tit. 3.5; Eph. 5.26. i.e. baptism.
-renewed by the Spirit]. Tit. 3.5. The Greek could be read as 'renewed in spirit' (as Wordsworth, *BSPB*, p.75) but 'renewed by the Spirit' fits the context better (cf. Tit. 3.5 in NRSV). Brightman ('Sacramentary', p.271, n. 11.27, 28) suggests renewal/recreation was a prominent feature of the Egyptian understanding of baptism, cf. Athanasius, *Epist. ad Serap.*, 1.9; Didymus, *de Trinit.*, 11.6.
-overcome . . . attacks of the malevolent powers]. The words rendered 'malevolent powers' (*antikeimenai energeiai*) are often used of hostile spiritual forces, cf. Justin, 1 *Apol.*, 44.12; Origen, *frag. 25 in Jere.*; Eusebius, *de Vita Constant.*, 1.31; Athanasius, *Vit. Ant.*, 51; Cyril of Jerusalem, *Procat*, 10; Basil of Caesarea, *de Spiritu.*, 38; *AC*, 6.9. It is the language of spiritual warfare. Cf. similar phrase in N.16.

from now on, the attacks of the malevolent powers upon them and the deceits of this life, and so be bound and united with the flock of our Lord and Saviour Jesus Christ and be joint heirs of the promises with your saints. Because through him be to you the glory and the power in holy Spirit both now and to all the ages of ages. Amen

[10] PRAYER AFTER THE RECEPTION[1]

Loving[2] Benefactor, Saviour of all who have made a conversion[3] to you, be merciful to this your servant. Lead him into regeneration with your right hand. Let your only-begotten Word lead him into the washing; let his regeneration be honoured and let it not be empty of your grace. Let your holy Word stand by him; let your holy Spirit be with him, driving away and throwing off every temptation, because through your only-begotten Jesus Christ be to you the glory and the power both now and to all the ages of ages. Amen.

[1] Gk. *analēpsis* (see below).
[2] Gk. *philanthrōpos*.
[3] Gk. *epistrophē*.

–bound and united with the flock]. This statement looks forward to the new Christian's full membership in the Christian community and solidarity with them.
–our Lord and Saviour . . . the promises]. 2 Pet. 3.18; Heb. 6.12; 9.9.

[10]: This prayer forms one of the group (Ns. 7.11) used in the actual initiation rites. Brightman ('Sacramentary', p.264) emended the title to 'Prayer After the Anointing' *aleipsis*) but Funk (*DECA*, Vol. II, p.184) retains the MS reading *analēpsis* as had Wobbermin (*Altchristliche*, p.10) whose reading was followed by Wordsworth (*BSPB*, p.71) and who accordingly renders the title 'After the acceptance—a prayer'). Cuming ('Thmuis Revisited', p.568) has 'Prayer after the Reception' as does *DBL*(p.75). Lampe (*PGL*, s.v. *analēpsis*) understands the term to represent a 'handing over' of the catechumen for baptism. Certainly the text of the prayer suggests it was used just prior to the actual baptism and probably followed an act of pledging loyalty to Christ.

–saviour of all]. 1 Tim. 4.10.
–conversion to you]. The term *epistrophō* implies a turning to new belief (in Christ) and a turning to a new lifestyle.
–this your servant]. This statement points to the specific use of the prayer with a catechumen undergoing the initiation rites.
–regeneration]. The term is used twice in this prayer and occurs in Ns. 7, 8, 15, 11, 16.
–lead him]. The term is *hodēgein*. It is used twice of Christ guiding the catechumen into the final act of initiation.
–with your right hand]. The reference is to Christ as is clear from the next sentence, cf. Ns. 3, 21, 28, 29, 30.
–not be empty . . . grace]. This petition seems to be set against the background of the epiclesis petition found in N.7.
–holy Word . . . holy Spirit]. Word and Spirit are closely linked here and both are seen to be active in the initiation rite.
–driving away . . . throwing off]. This language has an exorcistic colouring; *absobein* is used of driving off Satan by Chrysostom (*hom.*, 22.6 *in Mt.*) and *apoballein* is used of casting out a demon in Origen (*c. Celsus*, 2.49).
–every temptation]. The phrase occurs also in Ns. 24 and 25.

God, the God of truth, the maker of all things, the Lord of the whole creation,
bless this your servant with your blessing. Render him pure[2] in the regeneration;
appoint him a partner[3] with your angelic powers in order that he may no longer
be called[4] flesh[5] but spiritual[6], sharing in your divine beneficial gift. May he be
sustained until the end by you, the Maker of the world, your only-begotten Jesus
Christ through whom be to you the glory and the power in holy Spirit both now
and to all the ages of ages. Amen.

---

[1] 'Catechumen' has been added for sense.
[2] Gk. *katharos.*
[3] Gk. *koinōnos.*
[4] Gk. *onomazein.*
[5] Gk. *sarx.*
[6] Gk. *pneumatikos.*

---

[11]: This title is rubrical in character and indicates a prayer used straight after the
candidate comes up out of the baptistry bath.

It is difficult to be sure exactly what the post-baptismal procedures were in Egypt in
this period. (i. Kretschmar ('Beiträge der Liturgie, inbesondere der Taufliturgie in
Ägypten' in *Jahrbuch für Liturgik und Hymnologie* 8 (1963), p.39 has suggested the
evidence for the two anointings of Egypt in uncertain. However *CH*, 19
includes the two anointings of *AT* and adds a prayer which Bradshaw (*The Canons,*
p.24) suggests is so different from one in *AT* that it probably reflects local tradition. It
seems to me quite possible that the community which produced *CH* used two post-
baptismal anointings and prayer N.16 of *SS* seems to be very good evidence that at
Thmuis there was at least one. If there were two anointings at Thmuis, this prayer
would fit quite well with the prayer in *CH*, 19 between the anointings (though there,
and in *AT*, 21, it is accompanied by laying on of hands). Alternatively, it may simply
be a prayer said immediately after the emergence from the baptistry and would then
be followed by a post-baptismal anointing. It is fundamentally a prayer for blessing
and strengthening. Brightman ('The Sacramentary', p.271, n.1.9) associates it with the
presentation of the catechumen and proclamation of his name.

–Title—has come up]. Cf. Tertull., *de Baptismo,* 4 (*DBL*, p.8).
–God of truth]. Ps. 30.6.
–bless with . . . your blessing]. This petition expresses the focus of the prayer.
–in the regeneration]. The initiation rites are understood to effect purity.
–no longer called flesh but spiritual]. A statement reflecting the new regenerated
    nature of the candidate.
–divine beneficial gift]. Presumably a reference to the gift of salvation.
–be sustained to the end]. The prayer looks forward at this point to the neophyte's
    continuing Christian life.

God of hosts, the Helper of every soul who turns to you and comes under the powerful hand of your only-begotten; we call upon you, that through the divine and invisible power of our Lord and Saviour Jesus Christ, you may work[2] in this chrism a divine and heavenly work[3] in order that those who have been baptized and those who are anointed[4] with it—with the imprint[5] of the sign of the saving cross of the only-begotten, by which cross Satan and every hostile power[6] was confounded and truimphed over—they, having been reborn and renewed

---

[1] Gk. *to chrisma.*
[2] Gk. *energēsai.*
[3] Gk. *energeia.*
[4] Gk. *chriomenoi.*
[5] Gk. *ektupōma.*
[6] Gk. *dunamis antikeimenē.*

---

[16]: SS is not a Church Order like *AT* and *CH* describing correct rites and procedures, but a manual of prayers. It does however, not provide a specific prayer to be said at the actual anointing such as we find in *AC*, 7.44 (*DBL*, p.31). In *AT*, 21 and *CH*, 19 the anointing prayers are very short and simple and it is possible that this was true in Thmuis in this period. N.16 is a prayer of consecration of anointing oil, similar in that respect to N.15, but here it is referred to by the term *chrisma*, whereas N.15 uses the term *aleima*. The post-baptismal oil was often sweet smelling (cf. *AC*, 7.44,*DBL*, p.31) and is sometimes referred to by the term *myron* which was a perfumed, sweet oil (Hippolytus, *Comm. Dan.*, 1.16 and s.v., Lampe, *PGL*). N.16 is placed with the other blessings for oil (Ns. 15 and 17).

-God of hosts]. Ps. 30.6.
-who turns to you]. The verb us *epistrephein*, cf. N.10, n.3.
-the powerful hand]. 1 Peter 5.6.
-power of our Lord . . . Christ]. 2 Pet. 1.3. Cf. N.15 'a healing and strengthening power'.
-work in this chrism . . . a heavenly work]. The petition is for Christ to effect a change in the oil so that it may be efficacious. Cf. the description of the prayer of blessing oil in *AC*, 7.42 (*DBL*, p.30).
-imprint]. The term (*ektupōma*) was used of the impression made by a seal. Here it is used metaphorically, referring to the sign of the cross as a baptismal seal (cf. Cyril, *Myst. Cat.*, 22.7 and s.v., Lampe, *PGL*).
-sign of the saving cross]. Making the sign of the cross was seen to be a powerful, efficacious action by the early Christians, cf. *de. Incarn.*, 31, 1-4; Athanasius, *Vita Ant.*, 80, 35 (see further F. J. Dölger, 'Berträge zur Geschichte des Kreuzzeichens' in *JAC* 1 (1985) 5-19; 2 (1959) 15-29; 3 (1960) 5.16; (1961) 5-17; 5 (1962) 5-22 and article 'The Sign of the Cross' in *ODCC*, p.1274). As early as the time of Tertullian (*de Res. carn.*, 8) it was being used in the post-baptismal rite.
-Satan . . . hostile power]. The prayer itself now affirms the power of the Cross. On 'hostile power' see n. N.17. The aorist tenses suggest a reference back to the point of Jesus' crucifixion and resurrection.
-reborn and renewed]. The statement affirms the significance of the initiation rites in the process of becoming a Christian.

through the washing of regeneration, may also become partakers[1] of the gift of the holy Spirit. And, being safeguarded by this seal, may remain steadfast and unchangeable, unharmed and safe[2], blameless and unassailable, dwelling in the faith and knowledge of the truth to the end, awaiting the heavenly hopes of life and eternal promises[3] of our Lord and Saviour Jesus Christ, through whom be to you the glory and the power in holy Spirit both now and to all the ages of ages. Amen.

[12]: <This is introduced below, but the text begins overleaf>.

---

[1] Gk. *metochoi.*
[2] Gk. *sphragis.*
[3] Gk. MS *epaggeleia,* Brightman/Funk emend to the plural.

–the washing of regeneration]. Tit. 3.5. Cf. Ns. 8, 10,11, 15.
–the gift of the holy Spirit]. Acts 2.38; 10.45. The question of how the Holy Spirit was encountered in the initiation rites is a matter of continuing, lively debate, see S. Brock, *The Holy Spirit in the Syrian Baptismal Tradition,* Syrian Churches, Series 9 (Kottayam, 1979); G. Winkler, 'The Original Meaning of the Prebaptismal Anointing and its Implications' in *Worship* 52 (1978) 24-45 and a summary of the different traditions by Yarnold, *TSL*, pp.127-129; 138-141. The evidence here of *SS* seems to associate the gift of the Spirit with post-baptismal anointing. In *CH* the prayer by the bishop between the anointings seems to be a prayer for the pouring out of the Holy Spirit and is accompanied by laying on of hands.
–safeguarded by this seal]. Cf. 'seal' in N.9 and see n. N.19. The reference may be to the Holy Spirit or to the rite of baptism as a whole. On *sphragis,* see n. N.9.
–steadfast and unchangeable]. 1 Cor. 15.58.
–the faith and knowledge ... the end]. 2 Thess. 2.13; 1 Tim. 2.4; Heb. 3.6.
–our Lord ... Jesus Christ]. Tit. 1.2; 3.7; 2 Pet. 3.18.

[12]: It is clear from the carefully described ordination rites that have been preserved from the early period (of which those in *AT* are the earliest and upon which *CH, AC* and *TD* are all ultimately dependent), that they were regarded as being very important. Recent scholarship has led to both these texts becoming more widely available and to a much more informed understanding of them (see for example H. Boone Porter, *The Ordination Prayers of the Ancient Western Churches* (Alcuin Club Collection, 39, London, 1967) and P. F. Bradshaw, *Ordination Rites of the Ancient Churches of East and West* (Pueblo, New York, 1990) and the articles by F. Hawkins and P. Bradshaw in *TSL*, Ch. 4.). It is immediately striking, upon comparing the ordination prayers of *SS* with the other Patristic rites (*AT, CH, AC* and *TD*; the texts of all these, including *SS*, are printed by Bradshaw, *ORAC*, pp.107-126), that *SS* alone has no forms for any ordination/appointment to any of the minor orders, though we know from N.24 that there were at least sub-deacons, readers and interpreters in Thmuis. It is also striking that the length of the prayers is generally much shorter than those in the other Patristic rites, especially in relation to the ordination of a bishop. Perhaps the primary value of the ordination prayers from *SS* is that they reflect a tradition independent from *AT*. The prayers for the ordination of deacons in all the Patristic texts are discussed by Bradshaw,*ORAC*, pp.73-73.

Father of the only-begotten who sent your Son and ordered[2] affairs[3] upon the earth and has given rules[4] and orders[5] to the Church for the benefit and salvation of the flocks, who chose[6] bishops and presbyters and deacons for the ministry[7] of your catholic Church, and who chose[6], through your only-begotten, the seven

---

[1] Gk. *cheirothesia.*
[2] Gk. *diataxai.*
[3] Gk. *pragmata.*
[4] Gk. *kanones.*
[5] Gk. *taxeis.*
[6] Gk. *eklexamenos.*
[7] Gk. *leitourgia.*

Title—Laying on of Hands]. Cuming ('Thmuis Revisited', p.569) rendered *cheirothesia* as blessing even in relation to ordinations but as, argued earlier, (see n. N.28) there are good reasons for rendering it as here and I note after completing the translations that P. Bradshaw (*ORAC*, pp.122-123), in his translation of the prayers, has rendered the term in a similar way. Bradshaw (*ORAC*, p.34) has pointed out that, whereas in classical Greek practice *cheirothesia*, which literally meant 'the lifting up of the hands', was used to refer to the act of election of an office-holder, in early Christianity the term came to refer both to act of election/appointment and the act of prayer with laying on of hands. Later on as the laity's part in the process diminished the emphasis shifted so that the term primarily came to refer to the rite of prayer and laying on of hands (*ORAC, id.*). And this seems to be the sense of the term reflected in its use in *SS.* (On *cheirothesia* see further article by Turner noted in n. N.28 and Lampe, *PGL*, s.v.).

–Appointment of Deacons]. A further feature of *SS* different from *AT* and its dependent rites is that the ordination of deacons is placed first of the three orders of bishop, presbyter and deacon. This may simply be a grouping in order of hierarchy, but it at least reflects independence from *AT* (and *CH*). The term *katastasis* is used in the title of each of the three prayers but within the prayers the imperative *katastēson* is used of the appointing of the deacon, whereas *poiēson* is used of the making of the bishop.

–rules and orders]. The term 'rules' (*kanones*) seems to be used here in the sense of individual regulations or canons (cf. Athanasius, *ep. encycl.*, 2). 'Orders' (*taxeis*) begins to be used in the sense of clerical orders from at least the time of the beginning of the fourth century (Lampe, *PGL*, s.v.) and this seems to be the meaning in this context.

–flocks]. Gk. *poimnia.* The plural presumably refers to individual Christian communities within the wider catholic Church, focused around the local bishop.

–. . . your Son . . . who chose . . . bishops . . . presbyters . . . deacons]. Christ is seen to have established the orders and is the one who ultimately chooses individuals to fill them as they are called. There is no hint here of a part in ministry played by any minor orders though, as noted above, several minor orders are referred to in N.28. A clear distinction in the offices of bishop, presbyter and deacon and the minor orders is indicated in *AT* (2-14) and presumably this basic distinction had meant that at Thmuis, while there were minor orders, a special form of appointment was not seen to be necessary (on Minor Orders, see *ORAC*, pp.93-103).

–the ministry] <The note is on page 43 opposite>

deacons and freely granted[1] to them holy Spirit. Appoint[2] also this person a deacon[3] of your catholic Church and give to him a spirit of knowledge and discernment in order that he may be able[4] to serve in this ministry[5] in the midst of your holy people in purity and blamelessly, through your only-begotten Jesus Christ through whom be to you the glory and the power in holy Spirit both now and to all the ages of ages. Amen.

[13] LAYING ON OF HANDS OF THE APPOINTMENT OF PRESBYTERS
We stretch out the hand Master, God of heaven, Father of your only-begotten,

---

[1] Gk. *charisamenos.*
[2] Gk. *katastēsai.*
[3] Gk. *diakonos.*
[4] Gk. *diakonein.*
[5] Gk. *leitourgia.*

–the ministry]. The word *leitourgia* had a background in the Hellenistic world for acts of public service or of service to the community (*LSJ*, s.v. and J. G. Davies, *A Select Liturgical Lexicon* [Lutterworth, London, 1965]). It is gradually applied to Christian service and worship and especially the Eucharist. The reference here seems to be to the ministry provided through and by the three orders.

–seven deacons]. A reference to the selection of the seven deacons in Acts 6.3. In *CH*, 5 and in *AC* 8.18 the model for the diaconate is Stephen, one of the first seven deacons but in *AT* 8 the diaconate of Acts is not mentioned. Bradshaw observes that the model in *AT* 8 the diaconate of Acts is not mentioned. Bradshaw observes that the model in *AT* is more upon that of the servant-hood of Christ whereas *SS* seems to combine elements of both servant hood and the Acts-deacon model (see Bradshaw, *ORAC*, 73-75)

–granted . . . holy Spirit]. Acts 6.3-5 emphasizes that the seven were men full of the Holy Spirit.

–Appointment also this person]. Cuming (*Hippolytus*, p.13) observes that the Sahadic text of *AT* uses not 'ordain' as the Latin does, but '*kathistenai*', 'appoint' and the appointment of the deacon is made explicit in *AC*, 8.17 (*ORAC*, p.115) though in *CH*, 5 both terms are used.

–spirit of knowledge and discernment]. Is. 11.2; 1 Cor. 12.10. Neither of these qualities are used in the prayer for the bishop. In the prayer for the presbyter 'wisdom and knowedge' are sought.

–serve . . . in midst of your holy people]. The gifts are given for service.

[11] <The Introduction to N.11 is on page 44 overleaf>
–We stretch out the hand . . . upon this man] In the ordination of a presbyter in *AT* 7, the bishop lays hands on the presbyter and the other presbyters present 'touch him' and it is possible that this phrase here 'we stretch out' may imply that, in the community behind these prayers, there was a similar practice.

–God of heaven] Neh. 1.4.

upon this man and we pray that the Spirit of Truth may descend[1] upon him. Grant to him insight[2] and knowledge and a good heart. Let divine Spirit[3] be in him in order that he may be able to govern[4] your people and to be an

---

[1] Gk. *epidēmēsai.*
[2] Gk. *phronēsis.*
[3] Gk. *pneuma theion.*
[4] Gk. *oikonomēsai.*

---

[11]: In this prayer for the presbyter's ordination there is an explicit reference to the stretching out of hands upon the presbyter and this contrasts sharply with the deacon's prayer. Whether this is intended to reflect a fundamentally different understanding of their roles, it is difficult to be sure, particularly as this reference is also absent from the prayer for the ordination of the bishop. It may be that it is an indication that the whole presbyteral college participated in the laying on of hands (See Brightman, 'Sacramentary', pp.258-259). Certainly the prayers are rather different in their emphases. There is no reference to 'rules and orders' or to the threefold ministry in this prayer. There is also a much greater emphasis upon the Spirit and the reception of the Spirit in the presbyter's ordination. Bradshaw (*ORAC*, p.63) has suggested that the focus of this prayer is really upon the presbyter's role in the teaching ministry and that this prayer must have been composed in a period before the rise of Arianism led to a ban on preaching by presbyters in Alexandria. The presbyter is to commend the teachings of the faith and to be a reconciler as well as to have knowledge, wisdom, and an orthodox or right faith. These ideas also appear in N.25 (the prayer for the Bishop and the Church), and in N.19 there is emphasis upon the learning and correct interpretation of the scriptures. In common with all the prayers for the ordination of a presbyter in *AT*, *AC* and *TD* (in *CH* the prayer is meant to be the same as that of the prayer for the bishop), and in this prayer also the presbyters are seen to be successors of Moses choosing the seventy elders in Num. 11.16-25. On this prayer and the similar Patristic ones, see *ORAC*, pp.63-64.

–Spirit of Truth] Jn. 15.26.

–may descend upon him] The same verb (*epidēmēsai*) is used here as we saw was used in the epiclesis of the Word in the anaphora (N.1). Here it is used in relation to the Spirit of Truth and there are some six references to the Holy Spirit altogether in the prayer. Clearly the activity of the Spirit is seen to be intimately related to the process that was going on in the ordination and there is a similar strong emphasis upon the Spirit's role in the equivalent prayer in *TD*.

–govern your people] The three central aspects of the presbyter's role mentioned are leadership, teaching and the ministry of reconciliation (see Brightman, 'Sacramentary', p.256). Bradshaw suggests that the prayer implies that there was no sense of the presbyterate acting a 'collegial governing body' (*ORAC*, p.63) and Brightman ('Sacramentary', p.256) observed that there was rapid growth of the parochial system in Egypt leading to a greater independence and self-sufficiency in the role of the presbyter.

–a good heart] Lk. 8.15.

ambassador[1] of your divine sayings[2] and reconcile your people to you, the uncreated God. You who bestowed holy Spirit, from the spirit of Moses, upon those chosen; apportion[3] also holy Spirit, from the Spirit of the only-begotten, to this man, for the grace of wisdom and knowledge and an orthodox[4] faith in order that he may be able to serve you with a pure conscience, through your only-begotten Jesus Christ, through whom be to you the glory and the power in holy Spirit both now and to all the ages of ages. Amen.

[14]: <The Introduction begins below, whilst the text begins overleaf>

---

[1] Gk. *presbeuein.*   [3] Gk. *merisai.*
[2] Gk. *theia . . . logia.*   [4] Gk. *orthē.*

–to be an ambassador . . . (to) reconcile] 2 Cor. 5.20. The sense of the verb *presbeuein* is
    slightly awkward in relation to *ta theia sou logia.* The implication seems to be that
    not only will they be able to teach these things but that they will also live them
    and commend them by their lives. The 'divine sayings' indicate a reference to the
    scriptures, cf. N.25 where the reference is to 'the holy teachings'.
–from the spirit of Moses . . . upon those] Num. 11.17, 25.
–apportion also holy Spirit . . . to this man]. This seems to be a central petition of the
    prayer, cf. *TD*—'bestow your unfailing Spirit upon him' (*ORAC,* p.119).
–wisdom, knowledge . . . faith] 1 Cor. 12.8, 9. A series of biblical references highlight
    some of the fundamental qualities seen to be required of the presbyter.
–pure conscience] 1 Tim. 2.9; 2 Tim. 1.3.

[14]: In the early Church, ordination to the episcopate involved two basic processes—
the election of the candidate and prayer for the equipping of the candidate with the
necessary gifts of office. From the mid-third century the approval of a candidate by
the neighbouring bishops was required and several bishops therefore became
involved with the rite. The Council of Nicaea permitted a bishop to assent in writing
as long as at least three bishops attended the ordination (see Bradshaw, *TSL,* pp.357-
358). Brightman ('Sacramentary', p.259) observes that for the election of a bishop in
Egypt it was necessary to have the approval of Egyptian bishops, the clergy of the
vacant diocese and the laity of the diocese (see further Sozomen, *HE,* 1.24;
Athanasius, *Apol. c. Arianos,* 6, 30; Theodotus, *HE,* 4.22). Although there were some
specific procedures that related to the office in Alexandria, it can be assumed that
these three elements would need to have been satisfied in Thmuis and other regional
dioceses in this period. *AC* 8.4 provides a description of the processes that apparently
operated in Syria and it is possible to discern there the operation of basically similar
procedures.
    The most obvious feature of the episcopal ordination prayer in *SS,* when it is com-
pared with the other similar prayers in *AT, CH, AC,* and *TD,* is its brevity, and
Bradshaw (*ORAC,* p.46) has noted that its especial value lies in the fact that it represents an independent tradition from the others which are all related to some degree.
There is no reference in it to OT imagery such as we find in the other prayers, and
there is no reference to the teaching ministry as there is in N.13. Nor is there any

(Continued on page 46 overleaf)

You who sent the Lord Jesus for the benefit[1] of the whole world, who chose[2] through him the apostles, who appoints[3] from one generation to another holy bishops; God of truth make also this man a living bishop[4], a holy bishop of the succession[5] of the holy apostles. And give to him grace and divine Spirit which you have freely granted to all your true servants and prophets and patriarchs. Make him to be worthy to shepherd your flock and let him continue in

---

[1] Gk. *kerdos.*
[2] Gk. *eklexamenos.*
[3] Gk. *cheirotonein.*
[4] Gk. *episkopos zōē.*
[5] Gk. *didochē.*

---

explicit reference to any liturgical functions such as the forgiving of sins or any role in healing the sick which is referred to in *CH*, 3 and which perhaps might have been expected in view of the interest of many of the prayers in *SS* in the ministry to the sick. There is no reference to the laying on of hands in the text of the prayer although the title implies it and it is explicit in the directions in *CH* and in *AT* and *TD*. In *AC* (and the Syrian tradition generally) an open Gospel is placed upon the head of the candidate and no reference is made to the laying on of hands (see *ORAC*, pp.39-44). Another feature to which Bradshaw (*ORAC*, pp.49-50) has drawn attention is the emphasis upon the apostolic succession of the bishop and his role as a guardian of the tradition. He suggests that behind this may lie a community troubled by heresy. A final matter to observe is the reference to the pastoral imagery which draws upon the model of Christ as the true Shepherd and is also found in all the other Patristic rites.

–sent . . . Jesus]. Jn. 17.3.
–benefit of the whole world] The incarnation is conceived of in a fully comprehensive way.
–chose . . . the apostles]. Lk. 6.13. The model for the episcopate is very clearly grounded in the calling by Christ of the apostles, as in all the other Patristic rites.
–appoints . . . one generation to another]. The Gk. term is *cheirotonein* could either be rendered as 'appoint' or 'ordain' but 'appoint' seems to allow better for the fact that Christ is seen as the one who ultimately calls and appoints. The reference to the generations of bishops underlines the idea of succession and the continuity of Christ's call to individuals to shepherd the flock.
–God of truth]. Ps. 30.6.
–this man a living bishop] The term 'living' is a favoured one in the prayers (cf. Ns. 1, 6, 20, 24, 25, 28). Perhaps the sense of the petition is that he will play a role that will be life-giving to the community he oversees.
–holy bishop]. Cf. N.25 where the petition states 'keep him beyond temptation'.
–succession of your apostles]. Again the link with the apostles is emphasized.
–give him grace and divine Spirit]. The prayer for the bestowal of the Spirit is a further central feature of all the Patristic episcopal prayers. Here 'grace' (*charis*) is closely associated with the Spirit.
–make him to be worthy]. This is a further common idea in *SS*. Cf. the response to the ordination of the bishop in *TD*, 1.21 where the assembly cries out 'He is worthy' three times. This seems to be a variation on the rubrics in *AT*, 4 where the new bishop is greeted by all with a Kiss of peace 'because he has been made worthy'.
–shepherd your flock]. Acts 20.28; 1 Pet. 5.2.

the episcopal office blamelessly and without stumbling, through your only-begotten Jesus Christ through whom be to you the glory and the power in holy Spirit both now and to all the ages of ages. Amen.

[17] PRAYER FOR OIL OR BREAD OR WATER OF THE SICK
We call upon you who has all authority and power, the Saviour of all people, Father of our Lord and Saviour Jesus Christ. And we pray that you send forth a

-episcopal office blamelessly and without stumbling]. Again here emphasis is placed upon the quality of the life of the office holder.

[17]: Whereas prayer N.5 is a prayer of consecration in the eucharist of oil and water for the sick that have been offered, prayer N.17 is grouped in the MS with two other prayers (Ns. 15, 16) concerning oil and their consecration, but which relate to baptism. As noted earlier, Cuming ('Thmuis Revisited', p.571) regards all three as preliminary prayers of blessings of oil. Wordsworth (*BSPB*, p.77 and p.57, n. 1) described the prayer as a benediction and suggested that the oil may have been consecrated immediately before use. In other words it was a prayer to be used for blessing of these elements for the sick as the need arose. Brightman ('Sacramentary', p.261) also saw it as a prayer for consecration but, whereas the oil and water of N.5 would have been for private use, those blessed in N.17 were for the 'general purposes of the Church'.

There is no prayer for administration of the elements for the sick in *SS* (as is the case for pre-baptismal anointing, if we take N.17 as purely a prayer of consecration) but the words later in the prayer 'these your servants' are rather unexpected in a prayer that was purely a consecration prayer. One possible explanation might be that the prayer served essentially as both a prayer of consecration and administration. In relation to bread and water no further words of administration would necessarily be required. And even when the oil was used in anointing, a prayer such as N.17 might be followed by a short statement of administration spoken extemporally.

It was observed in N.5 (notes) that there are consecration prayers for oil in *AC*, 8.29 (and water) and *TD*, 1.24 but both are positioned later in the eucharistic liturgy and parallel *SS* N.5 rather than N.17.

In more general terms prayer N.17 is important in adding to our knowledge of the early Christian understanding of illness and approaches to healing. Anointing with oil for healing had been practised since Jesus' time (cf. Mk. 6.13 and James 5.14) and there are many examples of its use during the fourth century (See F. W. Puller, *Anointing the Sick in Scripture and Tradition* (SPCK, London,1904), pp.153-171).

This prayer provides evidence that in this period (and I am not aware of any evidence for it prior to the fourth century) not only water but bread was blessed as a therapeutic agent. This prayer is examined from the illness/healing perspective in *CHANT* (pp.285-297). The terminology of the prayer suggests someone who had available an extensive vocabulary relating to the field of illness and healing. Two terms are used which are not listed in *LSJ*, *BAGD* and in Lampe, *PGL*, only at this point (see below). Puller (*Anointing the Sick*, pp.88-100) included an analysis of this prayer, but from a somewhat polemical angle.

-the Saviour . . . Jesus Christ]. 1 Tim. 4.10; 2 Cor. 1.3; 2 Pet. 2.20; 2.18.

-send forth a healing power]. This petition is the equivalent of an epiclesis. The focus is not directly the Word or Spirit but a 'healing power' (*dunamis iatikē*) though no doubt behind this idea stands the belief in Christ the Word as Saviour and Healer. Cf. the similar phrase 'healing power' (*dunamis therapeutikē*) in N.5 and see *CHANT*, pp.289-291.

healing power[1] of the only-begotten upon this oil, that it may become for those who are anointed with it, or partake[2] of these your created elements[3], for a throwing off[4] of every disease and every sickness, for a remedy[5] against every demon, for a banishment[6] of every unclean spirit, for a casting out[7] of every evil spirit, for a driving out[8] of every fever and shivering fit and every illness, for good

[1] Gk. *dunamis iatikē.*
[2] Gk. *metalambanein.*
[3] Gk. *ta ktismata.*
[4] Gk. *apobolē.*
[5] Gk. *alexipharmakon.*
[6] Gk. *ekchōrismos.*
[7] Gk. *aphorismos.*
[8] Gk. *ekdiōgmos.*

–this oil]. The simple term *elaion* is used.

–those are anointed]. The oil was evidently intended for use in anointing rather than tasting (for tasting cf. the prayer for blessing oil in *AT*, 5) and certainly this was the much more common use in Christian healing.

–or partake]. The prayer focuses primarily upon oil and might be used to consecrate oil alone but it seems unlikely it would have been used in this form for bread or water alone. The bread and water were eaten and drunk, now regarded as therapeutic agents (see C. Harris, 'The Visitation of the Sick' in *Liturgy and Worship*, p.477).

–throwing off]. This term, along with many of the terms in this very long sentence, has a distinctly exorcistic colouring to it (see *CHANT*, pp.291-292; 296-297).

–every disease . . . sickness]. Mt. 4.23; 9.35; 10.1. This phrase is cited in healing contexts in papyrus texts P. Turner 49 (*Papyri Greek and Egyptian*), pp.192-193; P.Oxy., 1151, 27 and B.G.U., III, 954, 11-12) and Athanasius, *de Incarn.*, 18).

–remedy]. The term *alexipharmakon* was rendered by Wordsworth (*BSBP*, p.78) as 'charm'. It is not only used in this sense however, and the absence of any other ideas in the prayers with magical associations leads me to think 'remedy' is a better rendering.

–demon . . . unclean spirit . . . evil spirit]. These references reflect the common conception in the ancient world of the ubiquitous presence of hostile forces (See P. Brown, 'Sorcery, Demons and the Rise of Christianity: From Late Antiquity into the Late Middle Ages' in P. Brown, *Religion and Society in the Age of Augustine* (Faber, London, 1972), 119-142).

–driving out]. The term here (*echkorismos*) is apparently a *hapax legom omenon*. The author is clearly drawing upon as wide as possible a series of expressions to encompass the complete range of possibilities.

–every fever . . . shivering fit . . . illness]. The prayer attempts to make a comprehensive classification of all types of condition—both of a physical, organic kind and of a demonological kind.

–good grace . . . forgiveness of sins]. The presence of this statement offended Puller (*Anointing the Sick*, pp.95-100) and he proposed, without any textual foundation, that it was an interpolation. It does not seem to me necessarily to imply a view that a simply ritual anointing with the oil would, in a specific way, result in forgiveness of sins.

grace and forgiveness of sins, for a medicine of life[1] and salvation, for health and
wholeness[2] of soul, body and spirit and for complete bodily health and strength.[3]
Master let every satanic energy, every demon, every plot of the adversary[4], every
blow, every scourge, every suffering, every pain, or slap or shaking or evil
phantom[5] fear your holy name which we have now called upon and the name of
your only-begotten. And let them depart from the inner and[6] outer being of
these your servants, that his name may be glorified, he who was crucified and
rose again for us, who has taken up our diseases and our infirmities, even Jesus
Christ who is also coming to judge the living and the dead, because through him
be to you the glory and the power in holy Spirit both now and to all the ages of
ages. Amen

---

[1] Gk. *pharmakon zōē.*
[2] Gk. *holoklēria.*
[3] Gk. *rhōsis.*
[4] Gk. *antikeimenos.*
[5] Gk. *skiasma ponēron.*
[6] Gk. *kai* added by Brightman and Funk.

-medicine of life and salvation]. A similar phrase (without *sōtēria*) is used in N.1
(anaphora) at the invocation of the Word in a context concerned with healing.
The word *pharmakon* is an important word in both medical writers (*LSJ*, s.v.) and
in the field of magic/socery (cf. Rv. 9.21 v.1.). There are no magical associations
here or in it other three occurrences in *SS*, and in the context here, it suggests the
author relates together ideas concerning healing and soteriology, something
found also in Irenaeus (*Adv, Haer.*, V. 12.6, see *CHANT*, pp.99-103).
-wholeness . . . soul, body and spirit]. This phrase, coupled with the next one, *eis rhō-
sin teleian*, suggests that the author sees health in a very holistic way. The concern
is for attainment of health and well-being that affects the total person. The
modern interest in this emphasis is not new. On the trichotomous formula 'soul,
body and spirit', see Brightman, 'Soul, Body, Spirit', *JTS* 2 (1900/1901) 273-274
and n. N.15.
-every satanic energy . . . evil phantom]. The terminology here is clearly exorcistic in
character. Does the underlying language here, and earlier in the prayer, reflect an
understanding that illness is, at least partially, demonologically caused?, see
CHANT, p.296.
-fear your . . . name]. The use of the name of Christ is a central feature of early
Christian exorcism (cf. Mk. 16; 17; Acts 16.18; Athanasius, *de Incarn.* 30, 32, 50;
vit. Ant. 63 and see S. V. McCasland, *By the Finger of God: Demon Possession and
Exorcism in Early Christianity* (Macmillan, New York, 1951), p.109 and n.
N.5.
-inner and outer being]. Gk. *apo tōn entos kai tōn ektos tōn doulōn sou toutōn.* The
expression again reflects the comprehensive nature of the petitions of the
prayer.
-take up . . . our infirmities]. Mt. 8.17. Matthew is himself taking ideas from Is.
53.4.
-judge the living and the dead]. 2 Tim. 4.1.

[18] PRAYER FOR ONE WHO IS DEAD AND FOR ONE WHO IS BEING CARRIED OUT FOR BURIAL.[1]

God who has the power of life and death, God of the spirits and Master of all flesh, God who brings death[2] and gives life[3], who leads down to the gates of Hades and brings back again, who creates the spirit of people and who receives the souls of the saints and gives them rest. You who change[4] and convert[5] and

---

[1] Gk. *ekkomizomenos.*   [4] Gk. *alloiōn.*
[2] Gk. *thanatōn.*   [5] Gk. *metaballon.*
[3] Gk. *zoogonon.*

---

[18]: This prayer is the only prayer of the collection relating to funerals, though we observed in N.1 that the dead were remembered in the anaphora and a recitation of names was made. Cuming ('Thmuis Revisited', p.570) described it as the 'odd man out' as far as its likely position in the original order of the MS was concerned, but he felt that it was not inappropriate for it to appear in sequence after the blessings of oils. N.18 appears to be a preliminary prayer. Wordsworth (*BSBP*, 57) suggested that it may have been said in the house of the deceased, prior to the funeral. This is also indicated by the use of the term *ekkomizomenos* which Brightman notes (Brightman, 'Sacramentary', p.262) is a technical term used in relation to a funeral procession. We do have a prayer relating to funerals in *AC*, 8.41 and some further funerary details are given in *AC*, 6.30. In *AC*, 8.41, the prayer is said by the bishop and the broad themes of the prayer are somewhat similar to the ones in this prayer. The prayers emphasize the contrast between the immortality of God and the mortality of humanity; they refer to the sins of the dead person with the request for them not to be held against the deceased, there is in each a biblical allusion to places of rest with 'Abraham, Isaac and Jacob' and a contrast made or implied between earthly life and the place of the rest to which it is hoped the deceased has gone. Brightman ('Sacramentary', p.262) draws attention to a range of other Patristic writings which make some reference to early Christian funerary procedures. In a letter of Jerome (*ep.* 77.11) to Oceanus at the end of the fourth century, we have a somewhat triumphal account of the death Fabiola. The letter however also refers to some of the funerary procedures of the time and a striking note is the singing and chanting as well as the use of Psalms and a procession which in this case, was very lengthy. With this detail should also be compared the information about funerary procedures in *AC*, 6.30 where it is noted that singing is to accompany funerals. *AC* 8.42 also refers to a commemoration for the dead person on the third day which was to be celebrated with Psalms, lessons and prayers.

–power of life and death . . . gates of Hades]. Cf. in these lines Wisd of Sol 16.13, 14; Num. 16.22; 1 Kings 2.6. As in *AC*, 8.41 this prayer begins by emphasizing the sovereignty of God over all life. Hades reflects the OT understanding of the shadowy place to which the departed went. Here it seems to be indicating, that in the writer's mind there is no place where God's reign is not operative.

–gives them rest]. In a world of frailty, death is often thought of as a place of rest.

–change . . . convert . . . transform]. These terms underline the contrast between the mutability of condition and the immutability of God referred to in the following lines. Because God is the subject of the verbs, they also point the work that God is doing in the lives of his people, bringing renewal and new birth.

transform[1] your creatures as is right and expedient; you yourself alone are immortal and unchanging and eternal. We pray to you for the repose[2] and rest[3] of this man, your servant (or this woman, your servant). Let his soul and his spirit rest in green places and in secret places of rest with Abraham and Isaac and Jacob and all your saints and raise up his body on the day which you have appointed according to your trustworthy promises in order that also you may bestow, with respect to him, the inheritances in your holy pastures. Do not remember his trespasses and sins, make his departure[4] peaceful and blessed. Heal[5] the griefs of his relatives[6] by the Spirit of comfort and give to us all a good end, through your only-begotten Jesus Christ through whom be to you the glory and the power in holy Spirit both now and to all the ages of ages. Amen

---

[1] Gk. *metaschemizon.*
[2] Gk. *koimēsis.*
[3] Gk. *anapausis.*
[4] Gk. *exodos.*
[5] Gk. *iasai.*
[6] Gk. *diapherontoi.*

-you ... alone are immortal]. 1 Tim. 1.17.
-repose and the rest of this man]. This is the central petition of the prayer expressing the hope that peace and rest will be the final outcome for the person now that death has come.
-this man ... this woman, your servant]. The prayer allows for the application to a person of either gender as we saw in N.15.
-Let his soul and his spirit rest]. Both terms *psychē* and *pneuma* are used here, presumably to underline comprehensively the non-material being of the deceased, cf. the reference in N.17 to 'body, soul and spirit'.
-green places]. Ps. 22.1; This allusion and the following one speak of the abode in the presence of God where it is hoped the deceased person will finally rest.
-rest with Abraham, Isaac and Jacob] Mt. 8.11.
-all your saints]. The reference points to a communion of Christian souls along with the Hebrew men and women of God.
-raise up his body on the day ... appointed]. Clearly expressing the Christian hope of the resurrection of the body at the consummation of history.
-his inheritances in your holy pastures]. This very pastoral image points to the Christian hopes and promises cf. N.17 'heavenly hopes and eternal promises' and *AC*, 8.41 'give him his lot' (*Ante-Nicene Fathers*, ed. A. Roberts and J. Donaldson, Vol., 7 (Eerdmans, Michigan, reprint, 1982), p.497.
-do not remember his sins]. 2 Pet. 1.15.
-Heal the griefs of his relatives]. This is a warm touch in the prayer. It is not paralleled in the prayer in *AC*, 8.41.
-the Spirit of comfort]. Cf. Jn. 14.26; 15.26.

Alcuin/GROW Joint Liturgical Studies

All cost £3.95 (US $8) in 1993

1987 TITLES

1. **(LS 49) Daily and Weekly Worship—from Jewish to Christian**
   by Roger Beckwith, Warden of Latimer House, Oxford
2. **(LS 50) The Canons of Hippolytus**
   edited by Paul Bradshaw, Professor of Liturgics, University of Notre Dame
3. **(LS 51) Modern Anglican Ordination Rites**
   edited by Colin Buchanan, then Bishop of Aston
4. **(LS 52) Models of Liturgical Theology**
   by James Empereur, of the Jesuit School of Theology, Berkeley

1988 TITLES

5. **(LS 53) A Kingdom of Priests: Liturgical Formation of the Laity: The Brixen Essays**
   edited by Thomas Talley, Professor of Liturgics, General Theological Seminary, New York.
6. **(LS 54) The Bishop in Liturgy: an Anglican Study**
   edited by Colin Buchanan, then Bishop of Aston
7. **(LS 55) Inculturation: the Eucharist in Africa**
   by Phillip Tovey, research student, previously tutor in liturgy in Uganda
8. **(LS 56) Essays in Early Eastern Initiation**
   edited by Paul Bradshaw, Professor of Liturgics, University of Notre Dame

1989 TITLES

9. **(LS 57) The Liturgy of the Church in Jerusalem** by John Baldovin
10. **(LS 58) Adult Initiation** edited by Donald Withey
11. **(LS 59) 'The Missing Oblation': The Contents of the Early Antiochene Anaphora**
    by John Fenwick
12. **(LS 60) Calvin and Bullinger on the Lord's Supper** by Paul Rorem

1990 TITLES

13-14 **(LS 61) The Liturgical Portions of The Apostolic Constitutions: A Text for Students**
   edited by W. Jardine Grisbrooke
   This double-size volume provides in effect two of the Studies for 1990, and costs double price (i.e.
   £7.90 in England in 1993).
15. **(LS 62) Liturgical Inculturation in the Anglican Communion**
   edited by David Holeton, Professor of Liturgics, Trinity College, Toronto
16. **(LS 63) Cremation Today and Tomorrow**
   by Douglas Davies, University of Nottingham

1991 TITLES

17. **(LS64) The Preaching Service—The Glory of the Methodists**
   by Adrian Burdon, Methodist Minister in Rochdale
18. **(LS65) Irenaeus of Lyon on Baptism and Eucharist**
   edited with Selection, Translation and Commentary by David Power
19. **(LS66) Testamentum Domini**
   edited by Grant Sperry-White, Department of Theology, University of Notre Dame
20. **(LS67) The Origins of the Roman Rite**
   Edited by Gordon Jeanes, Lecturer in Liturgy, University of Durham
   A collection of basic texts touching upon the origins of the Roman Liturgy.

1992 TITLES

21. **The Anglican Eucharist in New Zealand 1814-1989**
   by Bosco Peters
22-23. **Foundations of Christian Music: The Music of Pre-Constantinian Christianity**
   by Edward Foley
   This second double-sized volume provides in effect two of the Studies for 1992, and costs double
   price (i.e. £7.90 in England in 1993).

1993 TITLES

24. **Liturgical Presidency** by Paul James
25. **The Sacramentary of Sarapion: A Text for Students** by Ric Lennard-Barrett
26. **Communion Outside the Eucharist** by Phillip Tovey (December 1993)

THE ALCUIN CLUB

The Alcuin Club exists to promote the study of Christian liturgy in general, and in particular the liturgies of the Anglican Communion. Since its foundation in 1897 it has published over 130 books and pamphlets. Members of the Club receive some publications of the current year free and others at a reduced rate.

Information concerning the annual subscription, applications for membership and lists of publications is obtainable from the Treasurer, The Revd. T. R. Barker, All Saints' Vicarage, Highlands Road, Runcorn, Cheshire WA7 4PS (Tel. 0928–575 666).

President

The Right Reverend E. W. Kemp, DD, Bishop of Chichester

Committee

The Reverend Canon D. C. Gray, MPhil, PhD, AKC, FRHistS, *Chairman*
The Reverend T. R. Barker, MA, *Treasurer*
The Venerable J. M. M. Dalby, MA, PhD
The Reverend M. R. Dudley, BD, MTh, AKC, DPS, *Secretary*
The Reverend J. R. K. Fenwick, BSc, BA, MTh, STh, PhD
The Reverend Canon R. T. Greenacre, MA
The Reverend Sir Derek Pattinson, MA
The Reverend Canon M. F. Perham, MA
The Reverend P. J. Roberts, BA, PhD
The Reverend K. W. Stevenson, MA, PhD, DD

PUBLISHING PLANS

The Alcuin Club has recently made a three-year arrangement with the Liturgical Press, Collegeville, whereby the old tradition of an annual Alcuin Club major scholarly study has been restored. The first title due under this arrangement was published in Autumn 1992: Alastair McGregor, *Fire and Light: The Symbolism of Fire and Light in the Holy Week Services.*

The Joint Liturgical Studies (see the list on the opposite page) have been reduced to three per annum from 1992, and the Alcuin Club subscription now includes the annual publication (as above) and the three Joint Liturgical Studies.

Grove Liturgical Studies

This series began in March 1975, and was published quarterly until 1986. Each title has 32 or 40 pages. Nos. 1, 3-6, and 10 are out of print. Asterisked numbers have been reprinted. Prices in 1993, £2.75.